Bookends

The Simon and Garfunkel Story

27/5

Bookends

Patrick Humphries

The Simon and Garfunkel Story

PROTEUS BOOKS
London/New York

PROTEUS BOOKS is an imprint of
The Proteus Publishing Group

United States
PROTEUS PUBLISHING CO., INC.
9, West 57th Street, Suite 4504
New York, NY 10019
distributed by:
CHERRY LANE BOOKS COMPANY, INC.
P.O. Box 430, Port Chester
New York, NY 10573

United Kingdom
PROTEUS BOOKS LIMITED
Bremar House,
Sale Place
London W2 1PT

ISBN 0 86276 062 3 (p/b)
      0 86376 063 1 (h/b)

First published in U.S. 1982
First published in U.K. 1982

Design Adrian Hodgkins
Editor Kay Rowley
Typeset by SX Composing
Printed in Great Britain by Blantyre Printing and Binding, Glasgow

Contents

Introduction

"We come on the ship they call the Mayflower
We come on the ship that sailed the moon;
We come in the age's most uncertain hour
And sing an American tune."   PAUL SIMON, 1973

There were a number of reasons for writing this book. The songs of Paul Simon, and the music of Simon and Garfunkel, was very important to me at a time of my life when I needed it. I cringe now – as Simon himself must – at the poetic petulance of *I Am A Rock* or the intellectual isolation of *The Dangling Conversation*. But at the time, how right they sounded. As a writer, Simon's only limitation has been to meet his own scrupulously high standards, and it's been a fascinating process to observe and share.

Then there was the fact that there had never been a widely available, current biography of Simon and Garfunkel. The financial possibilities of this situation were immediately appealing! Their names ran together as easily as cheese and onion in the popular memory. But how many people who bought *Bridge Over Troubled Water*, I wonder, realised that just five years before they could have seen Paul Simon perform over a pint, get a bus home, and *still* have change from a quid?

Simon and Garfunkel's appeal was as broad as the Beatles' or Bob Dylan's, but relatively little has been written about them. I hope this book helps fill that gap.

Simon was never one to rush into a song, his writing has been characterised by the beautiful craftsmanship and delicate structure which sees him closer to an older, elegant, school of songwriters. At the same time, Simon and Garfunkel were very much part of the rock 'n' roll generation, they grew up with Elvis and the Everlys, came of age with Dylan, and went on to create a distinctive, influential sound. The success of *Bridge Over Troubled Water* saw them reach an audience far beyond that of almost any other rock act.

What is remarkable in their case is that their actual repertoire was so small. Simon and Garfunkel only had creative control over three of their albums, *Parsley, Sage, Rosemary And Thyme* in 1966, *Bookends* in 1968 and *Bridge Over Troubled Water* in 1970. Three albums, and yet · · · The foundation of that success was laid with *The Paul Simon Songbook*. Paul Simon alone, virtually unknown, in London in 1965. But the songs from that album – *Sounds Of Silence, Homeward Bound, April Come She Will* – were S&G standards for many years. It is a fascinating album, the sound of a young songwriter intent on conveying every nuance in the fine collection of his own songs. Like Elvis Presley's best work with Sun Records in 1954, the commitment to the music rings down the years.

But it took the flawless voice of Art Garfunkel to make those songs known around the world. And that combination of Simon *and* Garfunkel is the one people will remember, like Marx and Engels, like Lennon and McCartney, their names flow together. They have proved with their music that there is a lot to remember fondly. With their current reunion, I am sure there will be a lot to look forward to as well.

I would personally like to thank Spencer Leigh, whose book Paul Simon: Now And Then (Raven Books, 1973) proved itself invaluable. Spencer also offered much sound counsel and co-operation when he had every right to offer none. From him I learned much about the complex chronology of Simon and Garfunkel's career, as well as having him act as an invaluable signpost at several crossroads.

I would also like to thank the following for advice, albums, time and tea: Lon Goddard, Judith Piepe, Richard Wootton, Wally Whyton, Bob Woffinden, Chris Charlesworth, Roy Carr, Maurice Shannon, Martin Carthy, Robert Shelton, Liz Thomson, Dave Marsh, Sue Foster at Warners and Kit Buckler at CBS. The enigmatic bits (in the best Paul Simon tradition) are to Mark Smith, for helping break the sound of silence; Alannah Hopkin, for encouragement, and because a launderette goes a long way in the country. And, finally, to that silver-haired daddy of mine.

PATRICK HUMPHRIES, JUNE 1982.

Chapter One

Few people can say for certain what the fifteen year old Paul Simon was doing on the evening of January 28, 1956, but it's fair to assume that – like millions of others – he was watching Elvis Presley's nation-wide television debut on **The Dorsey Brothers Show**. Like so many of his generation, Simon was hooked on rock 'n' roll from the word 'go'. It was hard to idolise the avuncular Bill Haley, but the twenty-one year old Elvis, ah, now there was an idol.

The original surging power of rock 'n' roll cut through race, class and environment. It gave teenagers their own music, their own heroes. Black ghetto kids could get off on it, so could white, middle class kids from Newark, New Jersey, where Paul Frederic Simon was born on October 13, 1941. Simon came from a middle class Jewish family and he was later joined by a younger brother, Eddie. The Simons soon moved to the comfortable New York suburb of Forest Hills where Arthur Garfunkel was born on November 5, 1941. Simon's father was a teacher, who also used to enjoy playing bass with local jazz groups later in the evening (the "family bassman" of *Baby Driver*.)

Judith Piepe, who knew Simon and Garfunkel well in London during the mid-Sixties, believes that their mothers formed a friend-ship at an ante-natal clinic, and that the pair were friends virtually from the cradle. Both boys came from families who had a keen interest in music, the Garfunkels used to enjoy family singalongs round their piano and Simon was encouraged by his father to sing and learn the guitar.

Judith remembers Simon proudly telling her that he was local stoop ball champion at the age of nine. Because of his size, Simon was always keener to prove himself than the taller, restrained Garfunkel. "Paul was always the one who initiated things", remembered Judith, "Whatever puddle there was to fall into, Paul fell into it first. Paul, also, being small had to be more ambitious . . . A boy who is 5 ft 1 in, and a New York Jew *has* to be ambitious!"

Simon and Garfunkel first sang together in public at a school con-cert, where they precociously trilled through *They Tried To Tell Us We're Too Young*. Judith Piepe remembers Simon telling her that he and Artie found singing at parties and barmitzvahs was a better way of earning pocket money than washing dishes. The old folk song *Scarlet Ribbons* was an early favourite. Both shied away from the rigors of American high school life, finding solace in rock 'n' roll; Paul doodling with little tunes and Artie diligently scrutinising the Billboard charts.

It's hard to imagine now the assault the rock culture launched on the comfortably Eisenhowered America of the mid-fifties. There was the rock 'n' rolling poetry of Chuck Berry, Buddy Holly and Leiber and Stoller; the swaggering sensuality of Elvis; Marlon Brando's sneering biker from **The Wild One** ("Waddya rebelling against Johnny?" "Waddya got?"). There was the beat literature of Jack Kerouac and the teenage angst of James Dean, before his final, furious end in 1955.

Already discovering the joy of English, the young Paul Simon must have relished many of those early rock lyrics, particularly Chuck Berry (I could just imagine Simon writing a line like "Campaign shouting like a Southern diplomat" – from Berry's *Nadine* – around the time of *Me And Julio* . . .) Simon and Garfunkel were obviously influenced by the rock 'n' roll music pouring out of the New York radio stations. Indeed, as late as 1973, Simon was eagerly acquiring cassettes of fifties doo-wop groups like the Cadillacs, the Monotones, the El Dorados and Frankie Lymon.

Running parallel to rock's growth during the fifties were a number of other significant events. In December 1955 in Montgomery, Alabama, Mrs Rosa Parks refused to sit in the part of the bus reserved for negroes, which started Martin Luther King's Freedom Riders. Nineteen fifty-six saw Khruschev condemning Stalin's purges while Russian tanks rolled into Hungary. It was the year John Osborne's **Look Back In Anger** was first staged and the Suez crisis brought the Eden government down. It saw Elvis at Number One with *Heartbreak Hotel*. With the help of Malcolm Leo's **This is Elvis** film, Roy Carr's lovingly compiled **Elvis: The Sun Sessions** and Alfred Wertheimer's book of photos **Elvis '56**, you can begin to appreciate the sort of effect Elvis would have had on the impressionable Paul Simon.

Discovering their voices blended well together, Simon and Garfunkel's obvious influence was the Everly Brothers. Phil and Don Everly's formative years were steeped in country music and, in switching to rock, they were lucky to find two Nashville writers, Felice and Boudleaux Bryant, who kept them happily in the charts throughout the Fifties.

The Everly's hits were all centred around the turmoil of teenage love – *Wake Up Little Susie, Bird Dog, Poor Jenny, Cathy's Clown*. They were concise, touching pop songs, enhanced by the brothers' flawless harmonies. Their success, and influence, on pre-Beatle American pop was enormous, something Simon and Garfunkel acknowledged years later when they included *Bye Bye Love* on *Bridge Over Troubled Waters*.

Simon and Garfunkel did some local shows together, street hops, neighbourhood dances etc. Sensing that the world was not quite ready for the implied intensity of Simon and Garfunkel, they took the cartoon alias of Tom and Jerry. Art became Tom Graph and Paul was Jerry Landis (a pseudonym he was to revert to in later years.) It was never terribly serious, just Paul and Artie trying to be Don and Phil. Garfunkel remembered the two of them riding the subway from Forest Hills to Manhattan after school: "You'd knock on a door and there would be this weird freaked-out black guy or this very fat cigar-smoking Jewish businessman, and they'd be gruff and you knew that it was a really hard thing to get into. I probably would

never have done that myself . . . Paul had a lot of the drive in those days."

New York was the rock 'n' roll centre of the world. It was where Alan Freed hosted his influential **Rock 'n' Roll Party** radio show and where the songwriters' and music publishers' 'Tin Pan Alley' was situated. So great was the demand from the kids for records that A&R men were out literally scouring the streets for talent. Teenage stars were no novelty in those days, perhaps the best known was Frankie Lymon, a star by the time he was thirteen and a has-been at fifteen. Simon and Garfunkel persevered and were demoing some of Paul's songs in a studio when they were approached by a producer who promised to make them stars!

They almost made it. Tom and Jerry were signed to the Big label whose operations were only matched by the label's aspiring title. Simon recalled the occasion to Rolling Stone in 1970: "We were making a demo in Sanders Recording Studio for two dollars. They didn't even put it on tape; they put it directly onto acetate. You had to do it perfectly because you couldn't wipe it out." It was perhaps early occasions like that which made Simon and Garfunkel such perfectionists in later years when it came to recording – ensuring they got exactly the sound they were looking for, regardless of the time or cost involved.

A fair indication of Simon and Garfunkel's earliest recordings can be gleaned from their song titles – *Hey School Girl, Dancin' Wild, Two Teenagers. Hey School Girl* actually did become a minor hit, scraping into the American Top Forty on its national release. This success landed the teenage Tom and Jerry a spot on Dick Clark's prestigious **American Bandstand** on Thanksgiving Day, 1957. Topping the bill was 'The Killer', Jerry Lee Lewis, pounding through *Great Balls Of Fire*. They must have made a curious contrast, Tom and Jerry in their red jackets and crew cuts piping through their Everlys' influenced hit, while Jerry Lee wildly hammered *Great Balls Of Fire* into the ground. Unfortunately, one of the few **American Bandstand**s not preserved on tape was this edition featuring Tom and Jerry.

Well, if sixteen year old Paul Simon couldn't get to *be* Elvis, sharing the bill with Jerry Lee Lewis in his prime wasn't bad going. (The Elvis obsession was a theme Simon returned to in his film **One Trick Pony** nearly a quarter of a century later.)

Riding on the success of *Hey School Girl* and the prestige of appearing on television, Tom and Jerry played down the bill on a number of rock 'n' roll package shows. Incongruously they appeared at Harlem's Hartford Theatre with LaVern Baker topping the bill, and Simon playing his first electric guitar which he had bought specially for the occasion. Tom and Jerry's follow up, *Dancin' Wild* didn't do anything, nor did subsequent singles and Tom and Jerry split. No one shed any tears, they were just one of hundreds of acts who pepper the pages of rock history – 'one hit wonders.'

The fruits of those sessions didn't surface in Britain until ten years later when the Tom and Jerry tracks were issued on a budget label, Pickwick. The problems arose because the album boasted 'Simon and Garfunkel' on the cover, which showed a current picture of the duo (Garfunkel carrying a copy of A.J.P. Taylor's **History of the First World War** which was hardly required Tom and Jerry reading!)

Tom & Jerry 1957

Clearly the Pickwick album suggested that this was the latest musical statement from the thought-provoking Simon and Garfunkel, poor old Tom and Jerry didn't even get a mention anywhere. A writ was subsequently served and the album swiftly withdrawn. Some entrepreneur should try and acquire the album, and issue it as Tom and Jerry, as it is fascinating hearing the young Paul Simon utter such sentiments as "The teacher is lookin' over, so I got to whisper way down low/To say 'Who bop a loo chi bop'".

In a 1966 Record Mirror interview, Simon was particularly scathing about the Tom and Jerry days, calling their music "fodder for

Garfunkel carrying A.J.P. Taylor's **History of the First World War** mental eunuchs." He witheringly continued: "I'm ashamed of it. Fortunately, we made it under another name.

"If I refreshed people's memories they might well remember the disc. Anyway, it made me a lot of money and I got enmeshed in pop values. I thought that having a pop hit was great status. I wanted to be adored by everybody. By the age of nineteen I was very depressed. I thought I was over the hill, washed up already. I'd peaked at fifteen!" This was at the time that Simon was being pushed as a prophet of alienation, a rock poet. And although "folk rock" was the phrase of the time, it seemed as though Simon, and his audience, couldn't quite cope with the idea of this intense, lyrical young man having anything to do with so frivolous a subject as pop music.

Four years later, Simon had mellowed sufficiently to admit, again to Record Mirror: "If they'd released it saying 'This is Simon and Garfunkel at fifteen' it might have been interesting and I would have said 'Okay, that's me at fifteen and I'm not ashamed of it.' I made a record at fifteen and everybody wanted to at that age. I just wanted to be Frankie Lymon again."

The obvious influence on the Tom and Jerry album is that of the Everly Brothers (notably on the intro to *Our Song*.) The eight songs with lyrics dwell on the perennial problems of teenagers in love. Juke boxes, school hops and adolescent angst are the key 'themes'. All the successful ingredients for Fifties pop can be heard; the sensitive teen ballad (*That's My Story*), including syrupy sax solo. Records like *Two Teenagers* filled the airwaves during the dull, comfortable Fifties. Tom and Jerry's fans weren't worried about the bomb or Freedom Riders, their crucial problem was whether or not to kiss on the first date.

The Tom and Jerry album is padded out with two instrumentals, *Tia-juana Blues* and *Simon Says*. They're credited to 'Simon-Prosen', the latter was Sid Prosen, the man that signed the two teenagers to the Big label. They're forgettable, cocktail bar muzak, solely there to flesh the album out to five tracks a side.

Their comfortable backgrounds and stable families ensured that neither Simon nor Garfunkel met the same sad end as Frankie Lymon, dead of a heroin overdose at the age of twenty-six. For the black kids in the Harlem tenements, rock 'n' roll was the only alternative to basketball or boxing to get them out of the ghettoes. For them, rock 'n' roll was an escape. For Tom and Jerry it was a hobby.

Simon and Garfunkel eventually returned to school. Both were academically bright, and Tom and Jerry were soon forgotten as they both prepared for University. Garfunkel plumped for mathematics, while Simon's interest in literature saw him go for English. Simon settled in at Queens University in New York and, although a diligent student, he could not (would not) hang up his rock 'n' roll shoes. Also studying at Queens was a young Brooklyn girl, Carole Klein, who did okay for herself when she changed her name to Carole King, married Gerry Goffin and went on to record *Tapestry*. But way back then, the two artists responsible for two of the biggest selling albums ever were just two teenagers with a love of rock music. They took their enthusiasm one step further by cutting demos in various studios after classes. This 1958 duo apparently called themselves the Cosines, Paul played guitar and bass, and Carole played drums (!) and piano, double-tracking their vocals. One of their collaborations, *Just To Be*

With You, was covered by the Passions who achieved a minor hit with their version of the song, modelled strongly on the Cosines demo. With New York's innumerable, insatiable radio stations, the Cosines were kept busy.

Carole King was fired by their minor successes, and in meeting Gerry Goffin later in 1958, she found her ideal partner. With her rich melodies and Goffin's acute, evocative lyrics, they moved quickly into Broadway's "songwriting prison", the Brill Building.

There, Goffin and King were responsible for some of the purest pop music ever, songs like *Will You Love Me Tomorrow?*, *Up On The Roof*, *Take Good Care Of My Baby* and *It Might As Well Rain Until September*. The Brill Building was where shifting combinations of writers were installed in bare offices, bare but for a piano. It was there that during the years 1959–1963 such permutations as Goffin/King, Greenwich/Barry/Spector and Mann/Weil laboured to produce a series of pop classics. It was the rich period between "rock" and "pop", and it makes for fascinating speculation if Paul Simon had followed in Carole King's footsteps, and had become installed at the Brill Building.

Simon, however, remained unconvinced that Carole King could make a success of her writing. He told Rolling Stone in 1971: "She wanted to quit Queens and be a songwriter. I said 'Don't! You'll ruin your career.' She quit, and had ten hits that year." By such mistakes is rock history made.

Already the writing of Chuck Berry and Felice and Boudleaux Bryant had exercised a strong influence on the young Paul Simon, and during the early Sixties I'm sure he appreciated the quality of material pouring out of the Brill Building. Leiber and Stoller's songs for the Coasters and Elvis have a preciseness which didn't escape Simon's attention. The Coasters *Little Egypt* has the classic couplet: "She had a picture of a cowboy tattooed on her spine/Sayin' 'Phoenix Arizona, Nineteen Forty Nine.'" Now *that* is just the sort of line I could imagine Paul Simon relishing.

While Carole King found success on Broadway, Simon persevered with his studies, but still dabbled on the fringes of the pop business. He recorded under various aliases (as Bob Woffinden noted in the **Illustrated NME Encyclopedia Of Rock**: "Simon's recurrent themes have included honesty and deception . . .") During the early Sixties, Paul Simon cut singles as Jerry Landis, including *I'm Lonesome* and a light-hearted spoof called *The Lone Teen-Ranger*. He was also responsible for Tico and the Triumphs, whose 1962 single *Motorcycle* reached number 99 on the Billboard Hot 100! He also sang lead on the Mystics *Don't Tell The Stars*, and received a flat fee of one hundred dollars for the experience. Garfunkel also floated on the pop periphery after Tom and Jerry split, cutting a number of unsuccessful solo singles under the name Artie Garr.

But the music scene had changed. The Elvis that emerged from the Army in 1960 was no longer the cynosure for teenage rebellion. The wily 'Colonel' Parker had decided to transform him into – that dread phrase – "an all round entertainer", and Elvis set off on the treadmill of those awful films throughout the Sixties. With the deaths of Buddy Holly and Eddie Cochran, the ostracism of Jerry Lee Lewis for marrying his teenage cousin, Chuck Berry in prison and Elvis crooning *Wooden Heart*, rock 'n' roll had become emasculated, a

College days

travesty of the powerful release that had attracted the young Simon and Garfunkel. Like many of his contemporaries, Paul Simon drifted away from rock 'n' roll and its anodyne successors. The initial power had gone, but being young and eclectic in New York in the early Sixties meant that the young Simon was open to all sorts of music.

Tico & The Triumphs – Paul Simon centre

It was in Greenwich Village during the early Sixties that the seeds for the 'folk revival' had been sown. The Kingston Trio had reached Number One with *Tom Dooley* in 1958 which had been enormously influential. Bob Dylan had hitched down to New York to visit the paralysed Woody Guthrie, and songwriters like Phil Ochs, Richard Farina, Tom Paxton and Ric Von Schmidt were working the Village clubs that also embraced jazz, blues and the iconoclastic humour of Lenny Bruce.

For many, folk offered the opportunity to discover America's rich musical heritage, it also offered a viable alternative to the WASP pop of Pat Boone and Bobby Vee. It took Peter, Paul and Mary to bring Dylan's songs to a wide audience. Dylan's success in turn revealed his debt to Woody Guthrie, and Woody's disciples like Pete Seeger, Cisco Houston and Ramblin' Jack Elliott. That audience sought sanctuary in a past they were too young to remember and savoured

Guthrie's dust-bowl ballads of the depressed Thirties from the middle class comfort of the Sixties. In folk they found a spiritual home, a home they had never really left but were keen to return to. They savoured the topical lyrics of Dylan, Ochs etc, and provided the audience for Simon and Garfunkel's songs later on.

Simon told Record Mirror in 1971: "Rock 'n' roll got very bad in the early Sixties, very mushy. I used to go down to Washington Square on Sundays and listen to people playing folk songs . . . I liked that a whole lot better than Bobby Vee."

Running parallel with the folk revival was the growing Civil Rights movement of the American blacks. Coinciding with the white, middle class discovery of its own folk culture was the blacks fight for dignity and equality in a 'democratic' society. Following Rosa Parks stand in 1955, the fight for equality had spread out from the South like wild-fire. Martin Luther King's eloquence, the Freedom Riders, the Congress of Racial Equality, all were out to break down the invidious racial barriers. As Dave Laing stated in **The Electric Muse**: "In a sense, the power of the revival was the result of the unlikely coincidence of Martin Luther King and Frankie Avalon!"

But if any one figure could be said to have popularised the revival, it has to be Bob Dylan. Reared on Guthrie, Hank Williams and Leadbelly, Dylan also recognised the rock 'n' roll heritage of Elvis, Little Richard and Jerry Lee Lewis. It was Dylan that gave pop music a voice, who brought poetry to rock 'n' roll. His first – rapidly deleted – single, *Mixed Up Confusion*, was a slab of rockabilly but, at the time pop was dwelling on the significance of an *Itsy Bitsy Teenie Weenie Yellow Polka Dot Bikini*, Dylan was writing caustic anthems like *Blowin' In The Wind*. His importance cannot be over-estimated. It was Dylan who ploughed the path Paul Simon would eventually follow. It was a debt Simon willingly acknowledged, as in this 1968 radio interview: "Bob Dylan was an influence on my writing. Before he came around, there was nobody writing the truth. No one was writing what they perceived as the truth, everybody was writing what they thought the audience wanted to hear. Dylan came out and wrote songs about himself . . . That was a revolution. That you could say the truth, and you could say it in the way you wanted to say it. For me, when Dylan put that down, that made it possible for *The Sounds of Silence* to be a hit. He made it possible for a whole group of lyricists to come onto the scene. I just think we wouldn't be there if it wasn't for Dylan."

Primarily to please his parents, Simon had gone to law school after university. Judith Piepe told me: "Paul's mother wanted him to be a lawyer or a doctor, and it's the old story that if you can't stand the sight of blood, you become a lawyer! . . . His mother told him 'Music's all very well Paul, but you can't make a living that way!' Famous last words."

But Simon's law studies rapidly took second place as he turned his energies to songwriting. His new songs, though, were removed by more than idiom from *Hey School Girl*. The political awareness in the songs of Bob Dylan and his contemporaries had a profound effect on Simon's writing. The song which marked his first effort at combining topicality with the folk idiom was called *He Was My Brother*, which was written during June 1963.

It was written about the young white kids who were going down South to stand next to the blacks in their fight for equality. It was this

version which was included on Simon and Garfunkel's *Wednesday Morning 3 AM* album the following year. But when Simon came to record it on his *The Paul Simon Songbook* in 1965, a more personal note was introduced. A friend of Simon's, Andy Goodman had been murdered by the Ku Klux Klan on a drive to enrol negro voters in Mississippi in 1964, which accounts for the change in the last line of the second verse in the 1965 version: "Mississippi's gonna be your burying place." (Tom Paxton also dwelt on the incident in his song *Goodman, Schwerner And Chaney* from his 1965 *Ain't That News* album.)

He Was My Brother was a touching, mature song, the final verse: "He was my brother/Tears can't bring him back to me . . . He died so his brothers could be free" . . . struck a note of optimism, which Art Garfunkel found encouraging: "There was no subtlety in the song," he noted, in his sleeve notes to the *Wednesday Morning* album, "rather the innocent voice of an uncomfortable youth. The ending is joyously optimistic. I was happy to feel the way the song made me feel." Garfunkel also noted that the song was "cast in the Bob Dylan mould of the time", but then, what wasn't?

Simon was encouraged by the strength of his first "proper" song, and continued writing songs which made up the bulk of his contribution to Simon and Garfunkel's debut album the following year. Garfunkel arranged several of Simon's songs for both of them to sing and, as Simon and Garfunkel, they performed *Sparrow* and *He Was My Brother* at Gerde's Folk City in New York in September 1963. It was the start of a professional partnership which saw their names irrevocably entwined for the next seven years.

February 19, 1964 was an important date in the life of the young Paul Simon. That was the day he completed his fourth 'proper' song, *The Sounds Of Silence*. Soon after that, with the summer vacation looming, Simon took himself and his guitar, and drifted over the seas to England.

Chapter Two

On the surface, Britain in 1964 was hysterically celebrating Beatle-mania; icons of the Fab Four were everywhere. Less publicised was the burgeoning interest in folk music in clubs up and down the country. An interest which was, ironically, sparked off by the American folk revival, what Robin Denselow has called "Dem East Croydon Blues". The incongruity of, say, a Hampstead bank clerk singing blues or dust bowl ballads went largely un-noticed by audiences fired by Dylan. Folk clubs in the Sixties offered a gamut of music, aside from hallowed renditions of traditional songs (so much purer than the dreadful pop music!) they also offered a floor for contemporary singer/songwriters. Bert Jansch, Al Stewart, John Renbourn and Davy Graham were only some of the promising British talent. Diz Disley was also in there, a guitarist who effortlessly crossed from folk into jazz (he was – as indeed was Simon – too deep for Django Rheinhardt when he played with the legendary jazz violinist Stephane Grappelli.) Disley is remembered in the first version of *Simple Desultory Philippic* on *The Paul Simon Songbook*.

It was a world into which Paul Simon slotted comfortably. Armed only with his guitar, and a growing repertoire of songs, Simon did a little busking, and innumerable floor spots around the country. As well as his own songs like *He Was My Brother* and the recent *Sounds Of Silence*, Simon also included versions of Woody Guthrie's *Pretty Boy Floyd*, Tom Paxton's *Can't Help But Wonder Where I'm Bound* and *Going To The Zoo* as well as traditional songs like *Scarborough Fair* and *The House Carpenter*.

Garfunkel had stayed in New York, supporting himself by tutoring mathematics in the early part of his summer vacation. He remembered, years later, that "It was like a little performance, you'd come into somebody's house and do your perfect fifty minutes. The game was never to look at your watch, but to *feel* what the perfect fifty minute thing was."

Simon, meanwhile, was revelling in the freedom that playing the clubs brought him and later confessed: "It was a great way to spend my time, I was roaming around in a small country where everything was new and exciting." Young was what everyone wanted to be in Britain during the Swinging Sixties, the youth cult was reflected everywhere, fashion, the theatre, cinema and music. In his travels round the country, Simon obviously fell in with other singers on the circuit. Al Stewart had hitched up from Bournemouth (after a spell as a guitarist in Tony Blackburn's backing band) and held down a residency at Bunjie's, just off the Charing Cross Road. Stewart also organised all nighters at Les Cousins, which was one of the key London clubs, along with the Troubador, Bunjies and the Scots Hoose. He also shared a flat with Paul Simon in London and spoke to me about those days when I interviewed him towards the end of 1980: "A lot of people, say Paul Simon or Bert Jansch, were influenced by Dylan . . . (They) were looking for a place to play. They couldn't just play at the Marquee, the Flamingo or the 100 Club because they wanted bands. But then, of course, if they went to folk clubs with acoustic guitars, at the time it was Alex Campbell and Ewan Mac-Coll, and it was very hard for a contemporary singer/songwriter to find somewhere to go. I think that myself, and others of my generation, were more or less lured into folk clubs because we played acoustic guitars."

With London as his base, the young Simon tore round the country, putting in appearances at clubs in Liverpool, Chelmsford and Widnes. Widnes is a town on the River Mersey, a bleak, Northern industrial town, dominated by chemical industries. It has little to recommend it, save that one night, while waiting for the milk train back to London, Paul Simon wrote *Homeward Bound* on the station platform.

Simon also appeared at the Edinburgh Folk Festival in 1964, sharing the same bill as Long John Baldry, who towered nearly a foot and a half over Simon. He also appeared, way down the bill, at that summer's Cambridge Folk Festival. Wally Whyton remembers meeting Simon during that first trip. The first time was at a folk club in Chelmsford, when Simon was double-booked with Whyton and Redd Sullivan: "He came in, as high as a kite, and the three of us ended up doing a whole evening of rock 'n' roll . . . Leiber and Stoller, the Coasters, *Dream Lover* and stuff. There was no folk music sung that night. But then, I don't think there was ever any question of Paul and *folk* music. That was also the first time I ever heard girls scream in a folk club."

Whilst he was in England, Simon cut a single on the Oriole label for which he disinterred his 'Jerry Landis' pseudonym and credited the two songs – *He Was My Brother* and *Carlos Dominguez* – to his alter ego, Paul Kane (taken from Orson Welles' film **Citizen Kane.**) *Brother* would surface on subsequent albums, but *Carlos Dominguez* has never appeared officially, apart from on this rare single. The only person to have covered it is that well known folk polemicist Val Doonican!

The song borrows from the folk ballad in its construction, a Question and Answer song, with Simon as the song's narrator asking Carlos Dominguez ("an unhappy man") just why he's unhappy. The ambitious Mr Dominguez merely wishes to find peace of mind, truth, answers and love. It's a typical Simon song of his English period, full of questions, with no answers provided. One can imagine Simon's embarrassment if it were released now, but it's a shame that room couldn't be found for it on *The Paul Simon Songbook*.

While Simon was doorstepping round the English folk clubs, Garfunkel spent the remainder of his summer vacation travelling round Europe. Simon contacted him in Paris, and asked him over to England. They had already a small roster of songs worked out to sing together but, as far as can be ascertained, they did no gigs as Simon and Garfunkel in England during that summer. The only

Paul Simon in London's
Argyll Street

detail we have is of their last night in England. Both had gone down to the Flamingo Club in Soho to hear the Ian Campbell Folk Group (Simon was later to cover Campbell's *The Sun Is Burning* on the *Wednesday Morning* album.) But the group, for some reason or other, failed to show up. The promoter, Curly Goss, was desperate for someone to fill the slot. In the best Hollywood fashion, he noticed a young kid in a corner with a guitar. It was Paul Simon, who got onstage and sang *A Church Is Burning, The Leaves That Are Green* and *The Sounds Of Silence*. He then beckoned Garfunkel up to join

Writing on the underground wall?

24

him, and the two wove their voices around Simon's *Sparrow*. The crowd was, predictably, knocked out and it was at the Flamingo that Simon and Garfunkel first met Judieth Piepe, who was to play an invaluable role in promoting their career.

Judith was (and still is) a social worker in London's East End. She was born in Silesia but fled Germany soon after the Nazis came to power. She came to England just before the war, and settled in the East End in 1962. She was interested in folk music and was singularly impressed by Simon's songs that night at the Flamingo. Judith spoke to them both after they had finished playing, and learnt they were returning to the States the next day to resume their studies. Judith was convinced Paul's songs were important and, at her insistence, Simon agreed to return to Britain for a week early in 1965. After Simon and Garfunkel returned home, Judith worked hard on their behalf in England: "I plagued the BBC and said 'There is a young American songwriter, and he is *the* songwriter of our time, and something's got to stay here before he goes away again. He'll only be in England for seven days.' I just drove them mad, so they finally said 'All right, he can have a studio for an hour.'"

Back in America, their studies took a back seat, as the duo began hustling round the record companies with Simon's songs. The songs were sufficiently strong to interest Dylan's then producer, Tom Wilson, at CBS. Wilson recalled the circumstances years later: "I started working with these two guys, one who went under the name Jerry Landis and also the name of Paul Kane, and he had a buddy who he used to bring round my office . . . I said why don't we call them Simon and Garfunkel? And Paul Simon said 'Hey man, people might think we're comedians or something!' . . . Anti-semitism reared its ugly head, we wondered whether people would take issue with the name. So finally, Norman Adler, who was the Executive Vice President, slammed his hand down on the table and said 'Gentlemen, this is 1965. Simon and Garfunkel! Next case.'"

As is often the way with the record industry, when one artist breaks big, there's a rush to push similar artists in their wake. CBS were riding high with Dylan, and Simon and Garfunkel presented an attractive possibility to the company. There was none of Dylan's vocal abrasiveness, none of Dylan's overt 'finger-pointing' in Simon's songs. Simon's targets were unspecific. Dylan had been banned from singing *Talking John Birch Society Blues* on the Ed Sullivan Show in 1963 for fear of offending similarly right minded people. Paul Simon's songs presented few of those problems, they dwelt on subjects like the lack of communication, and their clean, collegiate image could be safely accommodated on CBS – "The Sound of Entertainment."

Wednesday Morning 3 AM is the first 'official' Simon and Garfunkel album. The cover shows two earnest young men in ties, caught in a New York subway station. It boasted "exciting new sounds in the folk tradition". The cover was nowhere near as simple to set up as it looked, as Garfunkel was fond of recounting. Every picture from the first photo session displayed a clearly legible slice of obscene NY graffiti, which ironically features on *The Sounds Of Silence*, where "the words of the prophets are written on the subway walls!" It was a theme Simon was to return to in later years in *Poem On The Underground Wall*.

The founding father of Rolling Stone, the respected critic Ralph J.

Gleason, supplied the sleeve notes, which favourably compared Simon to "other representatives of the new generation's songwriters" like Dylan, Ochs, Tim Hardin etc. The album sleeve also features a contribution from Art Garfunkel who provides a fascinating insight into the genesis of the five Paul Simon songs on the album.

Garfunkel's comments, though, do dip into a pool of pretentiousness which must have put a few people off, as in describing *Bleecker Street* with lines like "The second line touches poignantly on human conditions of our time."

It is interesting to note that both Simon and Garfunkel and Bob Dylan included *Pretty Peggy-O* on their debut albums. Dylan's version of the old Appalachian ballad is raw and rough, he savages it like a dog does a bone. S&G's version is soft and reverential, recognising that an initial early strength of theirs lay in their harmonies. They also included Dylan's *Times They Are A-Changin'*, emasculating the intensity of the composer's original with their harmonising. From the beginning, it was apparent that Simon and Garfunkel offered the acceptable face of folk-rock.

What cannot be denied, though, is the strength of those early Simon songs, of which the best known must be *The Sounds Of Silence*. As a phrase, it has now entered the popular conscience, and as a metaphor for the insularity of big city living, it is still a striking image. From the consoling welcome "Hello darkness, my old friend", the song's protagonist is clearly defined as a poet, an outsider. As those seamless harmonies weave around the tightly disciplined structure of Simon's poetry, there is a chill realisation of a potent new talent making itself heard. It still stands as a classic hymn of alienation, of a voice which has to exist in a city but finds no comfort there. Then the poet sees the crowds prostrating themselves before "the neon God they made", realising that their downfall is of their own making.

The inability to communicate is the theme of the song, although it touches other areas, of Simon as a poet, aware he stands outside the mainstream ("People writing songs that voices never shared.") The core of the song, though, is how people become immunised against each other, how they are unable to convey their feelings. I agree with Garfunkel in his sleeve notes, it is "a major work." It is also, ironically, one of their most requested songs in concert – thousands of people paying to hear a song about loneliness and the inability to communicate with each other!

The album does offer other potent indications of Simon's burgeoning talent, like *He Was My Brother* and *Bleecker Street*, although there is nothing else on the scale of *Sounds of Silence*. Otherwise, the remaining cuts are drawn from other topical songs of the period, Ian Campbell's *The Sun Is Burning*, Ed McCurdy's *Last Night I Had The Strangest Dream* and the traditional *Peggy-O* and *Go Tell It On The Mountain*.

Of the other Simon songs, *Bleecker Street* presents a series of acutely observed images, from the beguiling first line "Fog's rollin' in off the East River bank" through betrayal and poetic prostitution. The voices "*leaking* from a sad cafe", the shadows touching, conjure up a scene in Greenwich Village, with lonely voices striving to be heard above the fog of indifference. *Bleecker Street* also employs Biblical imagery, which Simon was to continue using in his songs,

particularly the "long road to Caanan", the long road back to
innocence. As a whole, the song is a precursor to the cinematic style
of writing Simon was to later perfect.

Benedictus was a song Garfunkel had researched in his university
library, which he thought would offer a florid opportunity for the
two of them to showcase their intricate harmonies. *Sparrow* was the
third song Simon completed, much to Garfunkel's satisfaction
("With *Sparrow* begins much of the style that characterises all the
later work.") It's a prosaic song, rich in Biblical language "From dust
were ye made and dust ye shall be." Personally, it sounds a little too
close to Donovan for comfort.

Wednesday Morning 3 AM was inexplicably chosen as the
album's title track. Its theme was one Simon returned to on the
Sounds of Silence album in 1966, under the title *Somewhere They
Can't Find Me*. Ostensibly a song about a cheap and unnecessary
robbery, Simon imaginatively sets the song on the night before the
robbery. With their voices intertwined, Simon and Garfunkel even
manage to make the image of girl's breasts gently rising and falling
unerotic. The key line, and one which must cause him rueful reflection, is "A scene badly written in which I must play."

As an album, it hangs together but, by including so many covers,

either the duo or CBS were hedging their bets and didn't feel confident enough in entrusting an entire album to a young, unknown composer. *The Sounds of Silence* was a remarkably astute, mature statement from the twenty-three year old Paul Simon. Regarding the remainder of the album, Bob Woffinden put his finger on its faults: "He and Garfunkel . . . clambered aboard the folk bandwagon, borrowing protest from Dylan, and harmonies from the Everly Brothers."

Wednesday Morning 3 AM failed to ignite America on its release in 1964 (Britain had to wait until 1968, when it was released to cash in on the success of *Bookends*. It is an indication of Simon and Garfunkel's later, global success, that *Wednesday Morning* – their lowest selling album – had sold more than any Rolling Stones album except *Sticky Fingers* by 1977!)

While Simon and Garfunkel sat in America, watching "exciting new sounds in the folk tradition" nosedive, Judith Piepe was working hard on their behalf back in England. She knew of Paul's 'Jerry Landis' single, and approached Oriole to see if they were interested in a Paul Simon album. But Oriole had been taken over by CBS. Judith had interested the BBC though, and Simon returned to England in January 1965 to play some club dates she had arranged for him, as well as a valuable hour's worth of BBC studio time. He and Judith went in and recorded a dozen of Simon's songs in an hour. But, according to Judith: "Nobody knew what to do with them. The Home Service said it wasn't family entertainment. The Light Programme said it wasn't light enough and the Third Programme said it wasn't classical enough." Eventually, the Religious Broadcasting Unit took a chance, and broadcast the songs on its **Five To Ten** programme. It was sandwiched between **Housewives' Choice** and **Workers' Playtime**, a story, a hymn and a prayer. Judith grouped the songs into three categories: *Songs Of The Brotherhood Of Man, Songs Of The Loneliness Of Men* and *More Songs By Paul Simon*. They were broadcast over a fortnight, and Judith preceded the songs by talking about them and their composer.

All the songs broadcast were eventually included on *The Paul Simon Songbook*, except for *Bad News Feeling*, which Simon wrote about the drug addicts Judith had had dealings with in the East End.

Simon's songs were a great success, particularly among the younger, 'radical priests'. Judith Piepe was snowed under with letters, most of which began "I don't normally listen to this programme, *but . . .*" Judith's idea of using Simon's songs in this way had a marked effect on religious broadcasting in Britain. While not strictly "religious", Simon's songs of that period contained many themes and images which could be incorporated into the Christian philosophy. The success of the programmes even extended to Tony Jasper writing a book **The Religious Content Of Paul Simon's Songs.** Many of the letters Judith received were from people keen to know where they could obtain the songs on record.

Judith eventually did interest CBS in an album of Paul Simon songs, and he flew back to Britain in May 1965 to record *The Paul Simon Songbook*. It was all done terribly quickly, at Levy's Studio in Bond Street, just one microphone to pick up Simon and his guitar. It was recorded at a cost of £60, and Simon received the princely sum of £90 advance. Despite the sparseness of the album, it should be stressed

Previous page: On **Ready, Steady, Go!**

CYRUS ANDREWS

how important that album was. The songs on it were the basis for Simon and Garfunkel's repertoire for many years.

Alan Paramor of Lorna Music had agreed to publish Simon's songs, at Judith's suggestion. "Alan was a sweet bloke, but very much 'Moon in June' type . . . Alan felt sorry for Paul, he said to me 'He's a nice little boy but, of course, these songs are much too intellectual and too uncommercial.'"

The fact that two producers are credited on the album belies the simplicity of its recording. Stanley West was a hangover from Simon's Oriole days and Reg Warburton was someone CBS put in to supervise the recording. Simon reverts to his Paul Kane alias as composer of *He Was My Brother* and *The Side Of A Hill*, which was apparently due to problems still associated with his Oriole contract.

Considering it's his first solo album, Simon's sleeve notes are curiously disparaging. "This LP contains twelve of the songs that I have written over the past two years. There are some here that I would not write today. I don't believe in them as I once did. I have included them because they played an important role in the transition . . ." *Which* transition though? From poppy Jerry Landis to the committed Paul Simon? From the (then) failed folk singer to the promising newcomer? "I start with the knowledge that everything I write will turn and laugh at me" hardly sounds like the first steps of a fledgling writer. It's a trademark of Paul Simon's career, that precise determination, every move is clearly defined, there is little left to chance in his development. The remainder of his sleeve notes consist of a contrived dialogue between Simon and his alter ego, which read like he'd od'd on Dylan sleeve notes, J.D. Salinger and Samuel Beckett. Judith Piepe also contributes commentaries on the songs, in the style of Art Garfunkel.

The Paul Simon Songbook formed the foundation of Paul Simon's live appearances for many years. It contains the classic hymns of alienation (*I Am A Rock*, *Sounds of Silence*, *A Most Peculiar Man*) and the haunting love songs (*Kathy's Song*, *Leaves That Are Green*). It's a crucial album in any understanding of Simon and Garfunkel. It's simple and direct, a touching testament to a writer who has found his voice.

The innate simplicity of the production means that the songs have to stand on their own merits, and any deficiencies cannot be disguised by lavish production. Simon's singing is earnest and intense for, without Garfunkel's harmonising, the songs take on an urgency. Of the many available version of *Sounds Of Silence*, this 1965 version is, I believe, the best. Simon is still resting himself with the song, none of the complacency which is apparent in later versions is there (just listen to the way he attacks the penultimate verse "Fools, said I . . .") What is apparent on this version is a young man, justifiably pleased with the song he has just written, intensely proud and determined that each lyrical nuance should come across. There's an endearing vulnerability in Simon's performance here.

Even the cloyingly insular *I Am A Rock* is bearable here: The poet alone, with his books and his poetry to "protect" him from the pain of love. It's a hollow, adolescent song, one which Simon never sings now. Wally Whyton remembers Derrol Adams frequently performing a song called *I Wish I Was A Rock*, which he is sure influenced Simon. Rather than the intensity of his "major works", it is the

CYRUS ANDREWS

touching, childish simplicity of a song like *April Come She Will* that never dates. Reminiscent of English traditional ballads – which was the most immediate impression the folk tradition made on Simon – it lovingly details the changing seasons while never sounding banal. A child's fairy tale, written and sung by one with the vestige of childhood's innocence.

Kathy's Song was written by Simon in New York for a girl he loved very much indeed back in England. The inspirational Kathy is pictured on the sleeve of the album, on the "narrow streets of cobblestone".

Kathy was a secretary from Hornchurch in Essex, and was, according to Judith Piepe "very special . . . she's the silent love of *Homeward Bound* and *America* . . . every songwriter should have a Kathy." Deceptively simple, the lyrics are imbued with a passion and commitment Simon was rarely to equal. The doubts which he expressed in his sleeve notes are found again here: "I don't know why I spend my time/Writing songs I can't believe/With words that tear and strain to rhyme." An eloquent song of separation, ending with the naked pledge "I stand alone without beliefs/The only truth I know is you." Despite the beautifully wrought lyrics, *Kathy's Song* evokes that feeling of vulnerability and loss felt by the composer. A love song for lovers everywhere separated by time and space.

Flowers Never Bend With The Rainfall, *Patterns* and *A Most Peculiar Man* appeared on later albums, and will be discussed in context. Simon's most strident vocal was saved for *A Church Is Burning*, a condemnation of Klan actions against negro churches. Simon's disgust at their deed comes vehemently across but he also manages to pinpoint a detail which other writers would have missed: "But all that remains are the ashes of a bible and a can of kerosene."

The version of *A Simple Desultory Philippic* differs slightly from the version of *Parsley, Sage* the following year. The Dylan parody in the middle is extended, with "It's alright Ma, it's something I learned over in England" coming from Dylan's own *I Shall Be Free* from his second album. *The Side Of A Hill* is a return to the childish simplicity of *April Come She Will*, with clouds crying and flowers growing. Simon returned to the song the following year, when he incorporated many lines from the song into the *Canticle* section of *Scarborough Fair*.

The Paul Simon Songbook was an impressive debut, if debut is the right word for what was already Simon's third album. The appeal of the album lies in its simplicity and intensity. As someone who became synonymous with the studio precision of his recordings, the Paul Simon here is believable and vulnerable. But the confidence was growing.

Simon decided to stay over in England, and consolidate the contacts he had made on previous visits. He told Rolling Stone later: "I had a lot of friends there, and a girl friend. There was no place to play in New York." As well as regular gigs at folk clubs, Simon also played at a number of prisons and borstals, instead of the usual Sunday morning sermon. Lorna Music's Alan Paramor introduced Simon to Bruce Woodley of the Seekers, who were just beginning their run of chart hits. Together they collaborated on a number of songs, two of which – *Red Rubber Ball* and *I Wish You Could Be Here* – appeared on the Seekers 1966 album *Come The Day*. The pair

An early UK TV appearance

also wrote *Someday, One Day* for the Seekers, which reached number 11 on the British charts in March, 1966. *Red Rubber Ball* was a top three US hit in 1966 for the Cyrkle, an American group managed briefly by Brian Epstein.

The Simon/Woodley partnership was sadly brief. *Red Rubber Ball* is a catchy number, and *Wish You Could Be Here* is a touching ballad in the style of *Kathy's Song*. The sense of departure is defined by the intimacy of the surroundings: "The crackle of the fire is laughing in my ear/The room is warm and sleepy, and I wish you could be here." There's no chance of reconciliation and the song ends on a bleak note: "I think the winter's going to last a long time this year/I've got lots of empty time to kill, and I wish you could be here."

Another regular American singer/songwriter on the London folk circuit was the talented Jackson C. Frank, who also stayed at Judith Piepe's flat, with his girlfriend Sandy Denny. Simon produced Frank's debut, and to date, only album for EMI in 1965. Part of his CBS advance went into the cost of making the album on which the young Al Stewart played second guitar. To date, it has been one of Simon's very few outside production jobs. It was very much a one-take album, the vocal and guitars being laid down simultaneously, so the producer's job entailed little more than ensuring both started simultaneously. The Jackson Frank album was reissued on B&C in 1978 (with no producer credit) and it's still a fine album, containing at least one classic in *Blues Run The Game*. Bert Jansch was once quoted as saying Frank was an influence on the English folk scene, and it's a shame the album never received wider recognition.

Frank's sleeve notes on the 1978 reissue give an interesting insight into the plight of contemporary American artists drifting over to England in the mid-Sixties, and I get the feeling Frank's words could well have expressed Paul Simon's feelings: "I had just begun writing songs consistently at that point. I still remember someone saying 'Well, you are a singer-songwriter. Why didn't you stay in America? Look at Dylan.' And I replied 'The reason I didn't stay was that I looked at Dylan!'"

Dylan crops up again in a fascinating Melody Maker piece from September 1965, when the influential folk singer Ewan McColl had dismissed Dylan's lyrics as "old-hat" continuing: "They have no real anger – they've no more passion in them than ****Mrs Dale's Diary**!"

It was a controversial article, and the following week drew a response from, among others, "American folk singer" Paul Simon, who commented on his mentor: ". . . I do agree with the point about Dylan's poetry being punk and old-hat. I think it is just rehashed Ginsberg. Then again, he has written some very good songs." A grudging tribute from someone who, more than many of his contemporaries, benefitted from Dylan's songs.

CBS did release *I Am A Rock* from the *Songbook* as a single, which helped Simon gain some media attention, including an appearance on TV's best ever rock show **Ready, Steady, Go** in August. Ian Mann in Zig Zag remembered Simon being allowed on to sing his song, provided he deleted two verses to allow plenty of time for bill-topper P.J. Proby to sing his latest his *Let The Water Run Down*. Simon felt his song somehow more intrinsically valid than Proby's, and sang on, which meant the trouser-splitting Mr Proby had to be faded out halfway through his song to allow time for the adverts.

*a daily radio soap serial

But Simon was still gigging round the folk clubs, which provided useful spots for acoustic music although few of the contemporary singer/songwriters had any real links with the folk tradition. Hugh Jones of the Spinners refused to book Simon into his club in Liverpool, because he felt he wasn't "folk" enough, and that his fee of £5 was too high. Wally Whyton recalled the compactness and intimacy of the folk scene in those days. There was the indigenous talent, like himself, Redd Sullivan, Alex Campbell, Dominic Behan, Ewan MacColl and Peggy Seeger, as well as the visiting Americans, like Simon, Jackson Frank, Richard Farina and Carolyn Hester. Did he ever feel that the visitors, like Simon, were ever using the British clubs to further themselves?

"I think what we could give him was a very minute part of what he wanted, therefore he didn't demand a lot from us. I think he realised that the folk clubs were a blind alley but on the other hand, it was a way of meeting audiences." One of the last times Whyton saw Paul Simon was when he turned up at a club "Out of the blue, in a white Sunbeam Alpine, seven hundred quidsworth of sports car, when we were all running around in old Ford Anglias. He never said where he got the money from, but I assume it must have been the first royalty cheque."

Simon was very happy gigging around the folk clubs during 1965, in many later interviews he spoke fondly of those idyllic days. Although utilising little of the folk tradition, Simon was polishing his craft before appreciative audiences and learning from contemporaries like Davy Graham, John Renbourn and Martin Carthy. With two albums available either side of the Atlantic, Simon seemed happily resigned to the poor but happy life of a folkie. NME's Alan Smith interviewed him towards the end of his stay. The interview was not run until three years later, when *Mrs Robinson* was a hit but this 1965 interview does give an insight into Paul Simon's attitude at that time. Simon talks of the sentiments behind *Homeward Bound*, buying a Martin guitar, his "average sort of family" and ducks questions on self-analysis. Asked how he would cope with "a big pop scene with managers and agents", Simon replied: "I can't see that, no. I couldn't imagine myself in that scene. It's too competitive and it's too gimmicky. I mean . . . this record industry, it encourages freaks . . . I hope I never get to that scene where people will be just looking rather than listening. Rather than that, I'd prefer not to be known at all."

Simon speaks happily of his folk club gigs and his modest ambitions: "All I need is somewhere to eat and sleep, and buy guitar strings. I haven't any real need for money. So I've made out OK!" On how he'd cope with hit records, Simon responded: "Well . . . I've never had a hit, although over in the States right now, a song of mine called *Sounds of Silence* is beginning to move . . ." So was Simon, in the autumn of 1965 he went to Copenhagen to play some Danish club dates.

On the other side of the world, a CBS representative had picked up on *Sounds Of Silence* from the *Wednesday Morning* album, and was playing it to college kids, who felt the song had "hit potential". The general feeling was that it didn't have enough punch with simply two voices and an acoustic guitar, but it did have something. That something was brought to producer Tom Wilson's attention. And the rest, as they say, is history.

Chapter Three

Tom Wilson had recently worked on Dylan's electric, and electrifying, *Bringing It All Back Home* album earlier in the year. Protest was in the air, 'folk-rock' was on the airwaves. Wilson astutely recognised the potential in Simon's song and set about doctoring a backing track, using the same electric musicians that had worked on the controversial Dylan album. A further irony, when considering Simon's anthem to alienation, is that Wilson grafted the electric backing on without either of the artists being present.

There was no doubt that 'folk-rock' was the sound of the times towards the end of 1965 in America. The Byrds' *Mr Tambourine Man* had reached number one that summer and Dylan's own *Like A Rolling Stone* was just coming down the charts. 'Folk-rock' took literate, and frequently incisive lyrics, from folk and married them to rock rhythms. It was the dawn of a new era in rock 'n' roll. Simon and Garfunkel (and Wilson) made *The Sounds Of Silence* fit ideally into that market place. Its theme of alienation obviously struck a responsive chord in the vast American record buying public and the single made number one there in time for Christmas 1965.

Simon was in Denmark, oblivious of the song's treatment, and subsequent success. Chancing upon a copy of Billboard, he spotted *Sounds Of Silence* bubbling under the Hot Hundred. Rather than fly straight home to America, Simon flew back to England, and contacted Garfunkel by phone. As Simon recalled at the 1982 Reunion press conference, he was playing a folk club in Denmark the night he discovered *Sounds Of Silence* was a hit, and realised that life would never be the same for him again.

With the immediate success a hit record causes, Simon and Garfunkel found they were suddenly in demand. The same people that had offered them nothing but closed doors a few months before, now had open options and contracts to sign. Simon eventually flew back to the States and rejoined Garfunkel who was out of university for his Christmas vacation. They decided to do a few selective gigs to capitalise on the single's sudden success, then Garfunkel could resume his studies and Simon could return to England and live in style. But things were not destined to be that idyllic. Simon told Rolling Stone in 1970: "I remember the day *The Sounds Of Silence* was number one. We played in Pittsburgh, I think. We did a show on the bill with the Yardbirds, the Four Seasons, Chuck Berry, Mitch Ryder, Lou Christie and us. We sang *The Sounds Of Silence* and got paid 300 dollars for it . . . When that was over we said we're not ever going to go on stage again; it's ridiculous . . . So we said we'll just make records and that'll be it. Let's go split and go back to England and really live high. It never stopped after that."

Surprisingly, given Simon's standing in England, the record never made the charts here, until the Bachelors covered it in March 1966, of which Simon was particularly scathing. Understandably so, the Bachelors were never too discriminating in their choice of material, one song followed another. Their follow up to *Sounds Of Silence* was another song in the folk-rock, protest idiom – *Hello Dolly*!

A hit single obviously demands an album, *molto pronto*. The album was preceded by another single, Simon's Widnes-penned *Homeward Bound*, which made the American top 10 in March 1966, and the British charts in April.

The subsequent album, *The Sounds Of Silence*, was basically *The Paul Simon Songbook* with clumsy electric backings. Tom Wilson had left CBS and the album was produced by Bob Johnston, who was also producing Dylan. The haste with which the album was produced is evident in the choice of material. Six of the songs were available on the Simon album. *Anji* was an instrumental by Davy Graham, a standard Everest for every fledgling guitarist on the English folk scene. (Simon included the song to ensure the ailing Graham some badly needed royalties.) *Somewhere They Can't Find Me* was little more than a hastily re-written *Wednesday Morning 3AM* from their first album.

Of the new songs, *Blessed* was written when Simon was staying in Judith Piepe's flat. He had sheltered in St. Anne's Church in Soho during a thunderstorm and was fired to pen a song on religious cant and hypocrisy. The major new work was *Homeward Bound*. It's a classic song, perhaps *the* song about life on the road. Thomas Wolfe said "You can never go home again". Home for Simon here was London, and Kathy. He did return to that home but only briefly. We find Simon's initial distaste for his chosen profession ("But all my words come back to me in shades of mediocrity.") and the cry for comfort. The strict rhyming conjures up the dull repetition of the road ("And each town looks the same to me . . . And every stranger's face I see reminds me that I long to be, homeward bound.") The endless similarity and stifling conformity are characterised as ". . . A tour of one night stands/My suitcase and guitar in hand/And every stop is neatly planned/For a poet and a one man band."

It's more than just a saga of life on the road, the desire to return to somewhere you can call "home" is universal. Whether you're a commercial traveller or a poet and a one man band, being away is never as comforting as being there. Even now, with a limousine waiting outside the auditorium, and a jet to whisk him away, Paul Simon can still sing *Homeward Bound*, and can still make that essential message matter. That is the mark of a great song. It's also the mark of a great artist.

Richard Cory is noted on the sleeve "with apologies to E.A. Robinson." Edwin Arlington Robinson was a 19th century poet who wrote a sixteen line poem on the suicide of Richard Cory which ended with the lines "And Richard Cory, one calm summer night/Went home and put a bullet through his head." Simon expands Cory's character, and power. His workers envy his wealth, the orgies on his yacht and his political connections. But despite all that, the great man blows his head off, which just proves that orgies and yachts don't necessarily bring you contentment. (Them featured the song on their debut album, with a menacing vocal from Van Morrison.)

Richard Cory is followed on the S&G album by another song about a suicide. *A Most Peculiar Man* is altogether bleaker and more poignant. Both men die alone, one by the bullet, one by gas, but neither have achieved any degree of happiness. Judith Piepe remembers Paul reading a three line obituary in a London paper about a suicide, whose landlady described him as "a most peculiar man." "Paul thought it wasn't enough, so he sat down and wrote an epitaph for a stranger, and for all outsiders."

Simon introduces the disinterested neighbour, Mrs Riordon, and chronicles the man's isolation with a marvellous, cumulative use of: "He lived all alone, within a house, within a room, within himself." The "most peculiar man" is alleged to have had "a brother somewhere", whereas Richard Cory's death is news in all the papers. Two lives with nothing in common, save for their deaths.

We've Got A Groovey Thing Goin', as the title implies, is less intellectually demanding than any of the other new songs. Simon wryly notes it's "just for fun" on the album sleeve. Indeed, it recalls the frivolity of the Tom and Jerry days: "I never hit you when you're down/I always gave you good lovin', I never ran around." Which seems to cover that.

Given that *Sounds of Silence* was a hastily concocted album, its the album that helped establish Simon and Garfunkel. The original versions of many of the songs on the *Songbook* are frequently superior and Garfunkel's harmonies tend to diminish the brooding intensity of the originals, although his solo *April Come She Will*, the "child's nursery rhyme", is beautifully sung. Despite the gratuitous electrification, Simon's eloquence shines through.

I Am A Rock was reissued as a Simon *and* Garfunkel single in the summer of 1966, reaching number three in the American charts. It was an obvious follow up to *Homeward Bound*, the poet and one man band turning in on himself. "Friendship causes pain" is another reinforcement to the army of isolationists. In the cloying, self pity of the song lie the seeds of its failure. "If I never loved, I never would have cried," speak volumes for the writer's state of mind, and also find an echo in his audience. But the sentiments sound adolescent, and date far quicker than, say, *Homeward Bound*.

That summer of 1966, Simon and Garfunkel undertook a series of college gigs. Chastened by their experience of being marketed as part of a pop package, they honed their potential audience down to campus kids who would appreciate Simon's ambitious and literate lyrics. With many of the folk-rockers seen as one-hit wonders and Dylan in isolation following his bike crash, Simon and Garfunkel had the field to themselves.

Their next single was the ambitious *The Dangling Conversation* in September 1966. Its elaborate structure and flowery lyrics saw it fail to chart either here or in the States, ensuring that it would not be included in subsequent *Greatest Hits* packages. It was, without doubt, Simon and Garfunkel's most ambitious recording to date, the delicate plucking of the guitar, precise string arrangement and subdued drum give it a substance and quality their previous efforts lacked. Garfunkel admitted it was the song Simon had taken longest

Taken in the CBS Building in September 1966 – the month *Dangling Conversation* was released

to write, and was the song which had taken them the longest time to record.

Lyrically, the collegiate intrusion of "Can analysis be worthwhile/ Is the theatre really dead?" jars. But the intimacy of the surroundings are so delicately painted: "A still-life water-colour . . . As the sun shines through the curtained lace, and the shadows wash the room." One may cringe now at lines like: "And you read your Emily Dickenson, and I my Robert Frost," I can remember how impressed I was when I first heard the song. It was an impressionable age, and that song had so much to impress. Just the idea of a *dangling* conversation was somehow so suitable. All those tentative, teenage discussions, conducted amidst "the superficial sighs" on "the borders of our lives."

Enduring those adolescent traumas, that song seemed to sum up the whole emotional no-man's-land which had to be crossed. "We are couched in our indifference, like shells upon the shore" is a marvellous line, and "couched" is such a perfect word, posed and acute. I can still conjure up that room: Lined with books I never got round to reading, a foaming shore beyond the lace-curtained windows, to be explored, one day. And the conversation dangles, like all the great thoughts you never got round to thinking. Like all the emotions you meant to impart to that one great lost love. It's a tribute to Simon and Garfunkel that they can take a purely poetic line like "A poem poorly written, we are verses out of rhythm, couplets out of rhyme" and make it moving, and memorable.

As a foretaste of their next album, *The Dangling Conversation* was beguiling and showed how far they had already come. *Parsley, Sage, Rosemary And Thyme* eventually appeared in November 1966. The title was taken from the refrain of the traditional song learnt over in England. The cover showed Simon posing as a choirboy, seated with Garfunkel amidst a field of studio herbs, surrounded by prestigious Gothic script. Just the sort of picture college girls could hang on their walls.

There are many relics of Simon's days in England. *The Big Bright Green Pleasure Machine* was written about an all-night launderette in the Commercial Road near Judith Piepe's flat. Urged to write a song in the mode of the popular "beat" groups, Simon came up with this bitter, ironic song, with the killer line "Do you sleep alone when others sleep in pairs?"

Patterns is a step further on from *I Am A Rock*, the embarrassing "books and poetry" have gone, but it is still a man alone in his room, his life dictated by the patterns which shape his life. They are too big for him to break, and he's trapped, "like a rat in a maze", unable to alter anything. *Flowers Never Bend With The Rainfall* is musically lighter, but still is steeped in isolation. "I don't know what is real/I can't touch what I feel", emotions are a shield against harsh realities, only illusion keeps him going, he'll "continue to continue to pretend". With songs like that, Simon helped popularise the outsider, painting a remote, but romantic, view of the young poet, thriving in his isolation. The outsider has featured prominently in fiction, from Dostoyevsky to Camus.

Poem On The Underground Wall is in a similar vein, which came about from Simon's late night rides on the tube, coming back from gigs to Judith Piepe's flat in East London. "The words of the prophets are written on the subway walls", but here it's just one word, *that* word. With that effort, Simon makes it a gesture, a final, futile effort, the sort of gesture the most peculiar man might have made before his lonely death. "Slashed deep upon the advertising" it's a paean to graffito, the subway poet's stab at infamy, or immortality. The shuffling, subway rhythm of the song make it one of Simon's best ever, it's also one of his least known. Maybe the subject matter held little appeal for their audience.

Simon was obviously aware of his reputation as a writer, his sympathy for the underdog outsider. He told Jon Landau in 1972: ". . . Everybody says 'You seem to write a lot about alienation' . . . 'Right, I do.' 'Alienation seems to be your big theme.' 'That's my theme,' I said. And I proceeded to write more about alienation."

Judith Piepe recalls Simon's delight at having written a happy song like *Feelin' Groovy*. A writer should encompass all facets of human emotion and Simon was getting marked down as a permanent resident in the land of Gloom, on the East of Eden. The sheer exuberance of *Feelin' Groovy* is a delight, perfectly capturing that "dappled and drowsy" spirit he evokes. Of coming over New York's 59th Street bridge, content and tired, but not tired enough to sleep, conjuring up that sort of serenity which creeps over you in that pleasant state. Typically, though, Simon felt that *Feelin' Groovy* was an unsuitable Simon and Garfunkel title, and immediately gave it a "more intellectual" postscript, *The 59th Street Bridge Song. Cloudy* was another number in a similar mood, an effervescent song, which emphasised Simon's terms of reference at the time: "From Tolstoy to Tinkerbell". From a great Russian author to the one-dimensional heroine of a Walt Disney cartoon!

A Simple Desultory Philippic was an update of the same song from the *Songbook* the previous year. A tribute to the brilliant comedian Lenny Bruce who had od'd earlier in 1966. The Dylan jibe in the middle is still there and extends to the end of the song. Just as the song is fading, there is a thump, and Simon whines "I've lost my harmonica, Albert", which some people saw as a snide dig at what Simon saw as Dylan's reliance on his manager, Albert Grossman.

For Emily (Dickenson?) Wherever I May Find Her is a full flowering of Simon's poetic abilities, which *Dangling Conversation* demonstrated. Here, he was able to use words like 'organdy', 'crinoline' and 'juniper', like a proper poet! A lush, haunting song, that offers full range to Garfunkel's awesome voice.

The song for which *Parsley, Sage . . .* is probably best remembered is *Scarborough Fair*. As I wrote earlier, Simon had learnt the song in England, and was singing it during his 1964 visit. It's where he learnt it that caused considerable controversy. Martin Carthy was (and still is) the single most influential English folk singer of the time. He had been performing *Scarborough Fair* in his set for many years and included it on his debut album for Fontana in 1965. Carthy was a dedicated singer and discoverer of traditional material and exerted a tremendous influence on the folk revival. (He had helped Bob Dylan on his trips to England in the early Sixties. Dylan acknowledged that he took the tune for *Bob Dylan's Dream* on *Freewheelin'* from Carthy's arrangement of the traditional *Lord Franklin*.) Carthy remembers meeting the young Simon on those early trips and is certain the arrangement of *Scarborough Fair* was learnt from him.

Carthy told me that he remembers Simon coming round to dinner one evening with Tom Paxton, and writing down the words and chords of the song so Simon could learn them himself. When the song appeared on record, it was eventually credited to 'P. Simon/A. Garfunkel', implying that it was an original song, whereas Carthy felt the credit should at least have read 'Trad. Arr. Simon and Garfunkel.' A number of Simon's contemporaries on the British folk circuit felt he also should have cited the song's traditional source.

Judith Piepe, however, is convinced that it was Garfunkel who learned the song from an American student called Caroline Culpepper, who was endeavouring to teach Artie the guitar. One of the songs he practised with her was *Scarborough Fair*, which he later presented as a Simon and Garfunkel song. Judith Piepe remembered: "I know that Martin Carthy said that Paul had stolen the accompaniment from him. This is not true! . . . It is possible that Caroline had picked up Martin's accompaniment, it is possible that some of it came that way . . . I know that when Artie learnt it from Caroline, Martin Carthy was nowhere near."

However they chanced upon the song, it has since become one of the most popular songs in the Simon and Garfunkel repertoire. In the sleeve notes to his album, Martin Carthy speaks of *Scarborough Fair* as a song associated with death: "The herbs mentioned . . . (parsley, sage, rosemary and thyme) are all known to have been closely associated with death and also as charms against the evil eye." Woven into the Simon and Garfunkel version is *Canticle*, which is basically an adaptation of Simon's earlier *The Side Of A Hill*, the life of a child and a young soldier weighed against a cause "long ago forgotten" by the generals. (Scarborough Fair itself was a yearly event held in the north of England for over 600 years.)

Simon highlighted the breadth of the *Parsley, Sage . . .* album when he spoke to the New Yorker the following year: "Sometimes I make a song purely an impression, like *Feelin' Groovy . . .* It's a happy song, and that's what it was. There's the other kind of song, like *The Dangling Conversation*. It's intricately worked out. Every word is picked out on purpose, maybe it's English-major stuff, but if you haven't caught the symbolism, you haven't missed anything really."

There's that delight with having written a happy song but Simon also points out the "English-major stuff". It was an area Simon was palpably moving into with *For Emily . . .* and *The Dangling Conversation*. As he told Bob Shelton of the New York Times: "Pop music has become the most exciting area of all music today", but later admitted its limitations, and spoke of wanting to expand into areas beyond the three minute song, like the novel.

That is something which crops up in any evaluation of Simon's work, the Paul Simon Novel. As early as 1965 he was telling NME's Alan Smith: "I'm attacking it by doing short stories, and . . . developing character studies in the short stories. I'm treating these themes that I treat often . . . Isolation. Loneliness. Communication. By developing these character studies, I'll incorporate them eventually into this novel." He told Record Mirror in 1966: "Even at twenty two I think I've got quite a lot to say. And just the physical act of sitting at a typewriter gives me an intense thrill." Simon was, in fact, twenty five then, and we're still waiting for that novel! Simon did develop beyond the three minute song towards the end of the Seventies when

"New lyrical sounds for the sixties" – a promo shot from the Gramophone Co. of South Africa

44

he channelled his energies into the **One Trick Pony** screenplay. He did include a longish short story, *On Drums And Other Hollow Songbooks* in one of his early songbooks but otherwise there are precious few examples of Simon's prose.

In that same Record Mirror interview of 1966, Simon spoke of the sort of gigs Simon and Garfunkel were happy playing: "The college circuit is ideal for us . . . we can talk to the audience and communicate. You see, although teenage pop kids buy my records, I find it a little hard to communicate with them. We don't have that much in common."

Already, that hint of arrogance was apparent, with Simon priding himself on the quality of the material he was making available for the discerning audience. *Parsley, Sage . . .* was to be the last album of original material for 18 months.

It was during that silence that the accusation of rock poet was levelled at him. He did admit that *The Dangling Conversation* was vaguely influenced by T.S. Eliot, but around that time also remarked that it wasn't that his lyrics were *that* good; it was just that everyone else's were so bad! There is no doubt that Simon's lyrics have been consistently excellent over the years, he helped bring the discipline of poetry to rock, and the ability to convey shades of meaning and emotion in precious few words. His lyrics are rare in that they *can* be read apart from the music, so yes, Paul Simon could be considered a poet. But those words only achieve their full impact in conjunction with the scrupulously arranged music, harmonies and production. Together, they are all the more capable of evoking a response in the listener. From a 1968 interview, Simon said: "There's a difference between being a songwriter and a poet . . . When I'm writing a song, I'm writing it to be sung, not to be read aloud. It puts limitations on your words, your use of words . . . A lot of times, words that are sung in a song really make it, and when you look at them on paper they don't . . . But when they're *sung*, that's the added dimension that was intended by the writer."

A Hazy Shade Of Winter was Simon and Garfunkel's last single of 1966. An impressive record, with a driving rock rhythm, fascinating brass punctuations and, as expected, rich lyrics and harmonies. It marks the transition between the florid *Dangling Conversation* and the sparse *Overs*.

Hazy Shade finds Simon "in the springtime" of his life, yet finding his memory skipping over "manuscripts of unpublished rhyme." The sort of rhyme that recurs "in shades of mediocrity." As its title suggests, it's an autumnal song, with Simon moving into the shades of grey that maturity brings. The issues are no longer black and white.

The folk revival had seen its efforts rewarded by the vanguard being able to fill concert halls and campuses across the country. The 'British Invasion', spearheaded by the Beatles and the Stones, had made America aware of its own rock 'n' roll heritage where the first opposition to the government's escalation of the Vietnam war was becoming apparent. A vague sort of 'movement' was growing. A sort of mellow, nihilistic movement, which the front pages called the hippies and were so much a part of that summer of *Sergeant Pepper*.

Vague philosophies were distilled from Dylan, assorted other gurus, and drugs. The hippies gravitated towards two streets in San

Francisco, Haight and Ashbury. San Francisco's romantic architecture, benign tolerance and location meant it was the cynosure of all young eyes during that summer of 1967. The Grateful Dead, Jefferson Airplane and Quicksilver Messenger Service were only some of the bands that "played real good, for free" that summer. San Francisco's hippy rise was only matched in swiftness by its decline. It became the focal point for the youth of a nation which, on the surface, had everything. But where its heart was supposed to beat was an empty, gaping space.

American essayist Joan Didion captured some of that turmoil during that summer in her piece **Slouching Towards Bethlehem**: "Adolescents drifted from city to torn city, sloughing off both the past and the future as snakes shed their skins, children who were never taught and would now never learn the games that held the society together. People were missing. Children were missing. Parents were missing. Those left behind filled desultory missing persons reports, then moved on themselves."

At The Zoo was Simon and Garfunkel's first single of 1967, and captured some of that West Coast excitement, yet is tinged with East Coast disillusionment. Ostensibly a New York song, its sentiments are connected with San Francisco ("Someone told me it's all happening . . . I do believe it, I do believe it's true.") In that human zoo are contained all the stereotypes which make up our society. If now it seems contrived and elaborate, the structure sustains the song. The first couple of verses are straightforward descriptions of the journey on the crosstown bus to the zoo. Once there, the poet usurps the narrator. Simon, as a topical writer, could hardly help but notice the changes, and something *was* happening.

Chapter Four

Early in 1967, Paul Simon was asked to serve on the steering committee for the Monterey Pop Festival in California, along with Brian Jones, Paul McCartney and John Phillips. Monterey was the first rock festival and should have acted as a guideline for subsequent events. It was a communal, well-organised festival; a celebration of the new music. Scheduled for the weekend of June 16–18, 1967, 7,000 tickets were sold, and 50,000 people turned up. It was where the Who and Jimi Hendrix literally smashed their way into the American market, appearing alongside the Mamas and Papas, Buffalo Springfield, Janis Joplin and Laura Nyro. Monterey marked Simon and Garfunkel's only festival appearance, where they premiered *Punky's Dilemma*, just the two of them holding the audience spellbound, a quiet interlude from the flaming pyrotechnics of Hendrix and the Who. Clive Davis of CBS called the festival "a glimpse of the new world." Simon was pleased with the organisation and subsequent success of Monterey, he told Sounds in 1971: "I was in charge of some of the money from Monterey that was used to have guitar teaching in some ghettoes, scholarship things that I've helped to set up."

Simon and Garfunkel paid a brief visit to Britain in 1967, playing sell out concerts at London's Royal Albert Hall, Birmingham and Manchester. They renewed old acquaintances and proved how far from Widnes they had come. Simon was pretty scathing about the great British public's unwillingness to send any S&G records racing up the charts. He told Record Mirror's Norman Jopling: "The Seekers and the Bachelors . . . What kind of image are we getting with our songs being recorded by groups like that? Our version of *Sounds Of Silence* was far superior to the Bachelors but we didn't make the charts here – I think I write the wrong material for Britain . . . Take the *Dangling Conversation*, it just wasn't suitable for the British market, it was above the kids."

That sort of intellectual arrogance won Simon few new friends in Britain. The fact that one of the songs he'd written with the Seekers' Bruce Woodley, *Red Rubber Ball*, had reached number one in America the previous year didn't seem to matter to him. Simon's innate belief in his own material was apparent in that same interview: "I mean, us recording a song called *Feelin' Groovy*? . . . I thought, well, give it a more intellectual title, I thought of *59th Street Bridge Song* . . . I knew that record was a hit as soon as I wrote it!"

Such statements present someone not modest about his own abilities. Someone striving for intellectual recognition, and seemingly ashamed that pop music was the field in which he had achieved that success. That sort of intemperate attitude was one with which a number of people found fault and the phrase "Napoleon Complex" cropped up, the idea that – because he was so sensitive about his height – Simon had to keep proving himself. But even people that were critical of him as a person respected him as a writer.

Fakin' It was released in the summer of 1967 and cropped up the following year on *Bookends*. The B-side, *You Don't Know Where Your Interest Lies*, is a real curiosity and has never appeared on any subsequent album. If it had become widely known, I'm sure the song would have almost got Simon lynched by feminists. Early on, he informs us he is "womanly wise", and tells the woman in the song, the object of his scorn "You're just a game that I like to play." I'm sure the song is deliberately ironic, for, as Simon told Rolling Stone later: "I'm for the feminist movement . . . I believe that women are a group that is discriminated against."

Nineteen sixty seven was the year that marked the Beatles apogee with *Sergeant Pepper*; saw debut albums from Hendrix, the Doors, Country Joe and the Fish, yet had no new Simon and Garfunkel album. Dylan had broken his neck in the summer of 1966 and was recuperating in Woodstock. Simon was hardly charitable. From a 1967 interview he said: "Dylan is dead, he means nothing – because he doesn't release any new material any more." In San Francisco, in the autumn of 1967, the hippies carried a symbolic coffin through the streets. With the escalation of the war in Vietnam and the very real possibility of the draft affecting them, the kids realised that putting flowers down the barrels of National Guardsmen's guns wasn't the answer. Next year it would be Mace and clubs, with one more Richard Nixon to kick around.

Times and attitudes had changed, the establishment was hardening its line. Values were being constantly questioned, mainly through the medium of rock music. Film and literature were slow in catching up. A moderately successful novel by Charles Webb was published in 1963 called **The Graduate**. It charted those changing values but it took film director Mike Nichols to clarify that dissatisfaction. Nichols had first come to prominence in America with his partner Elaine May in the early Sixties, when the duo wrote and performed deliciously sharp satiric sketches. When the partnership split, Nichols went on to direct the film of **Who's Afraid Of Virginia Woolf?** with Richard Burton and Elizabeth Taylor. It won her an Oscar, and Nichols was suddenly hot. For his second film, he chose the unknown Dustin Hoffman to play the eponymous hero of Webb's novel. Nichols had heard his brother's copy of *Parsley, Sage, Rosemary And Thyme*, and approached Simon to write the soundtrack for **The Graduate**.

Simon had read the novel, and dismissed it as only an English major could as "bad Salinger . . . I didn't like anything about the film at first. I was only impressed with Mike Nichols who asked us to do it." Clive Davis at CBS thought it would be a good career move for the duo as well, and "grabbed" the rights for the film soundtrack, assuming Simon would come up with enough new material to fill it.

The song most associated with **The Graduate**, *Mrs Robinson*, wasn't even fully used in the film. Simon and Garfunkel saw some of the film's rushes and, as nothing immediately suggested itself in the

way of new songs, they decided to slot older songs in as a temporary measure, until Simon had got round to writing specific new material. But Mike Nichols was happy with the way that *Sounds of Silence*, *Scarborough Fair*, *April Come She Will* and *Big Bright Green Pleasure Machine* slotted in and decided to keep them on the soundtrack.

Simon and Garfunkel then went back to resume work on their next proper album, *Bookends*. But Clive Davis was worried about the soundtrack for *The Graduate*, which he envisaged as an album of fresh S&G material. Simon was emphatic that he had no more material for the album. It wasn't until Davis saw the finished film did he realise that Dave Grusin's additional mood music could be used to pad out an album which only featured about 15 minutes worth of Paul Simon songs. He approached Mort Lewis, Simon and Garfunkel's manager, with the idea, but neither he nor Simon or Garfunkel were keen.

All three felt that a Simon and Garfunkel album should be just that: 11 new songs, an S&G picture on the cover etc. Davis felt that the film soundtrack would help them reach a far wider audience but Simon was insistent, he told Davis: "We've been working on the *Bookends* album a long time, we love it, and we think it's a major creative breakthrough. We don't want to wait six months to release it just because of your commercial problems." Davis promised that **The Graduate** and *Bookends* would be released simultaneously, which would, if anything, enhance not only their reputation, but also stimulate sales. Eventually and reluctantly, Simon, Garfunkel and Lewis agreed.

Ironically, it was the success of **The Graduate** which commercially established Simon and Garfunkel, the album neither wanted released. **The Graduate** was one of those rare films which perfectly captured the feeling of the times, and spawned a whole clutch of derivative movies. A sparkling performance from Dustin Hofman, Nichols imaginative direction and Buck Henry's witty script ensured its success (to date it's taken over 50 million dollars in America alone). Simon and Garfunkel's songs certainly enhance the finished film, it's only a pity there weren't more of them. *At The Zoo*, for example, would ideally have suited the zoo sequence which even includes a ride on the crosstown bus! The soundtrack sold substantially, mainly to fans of the film who wanted a souvenir. *Bookends* sold to devoted S&G fans, who were growing in number with each successive album.

As an album, *Bookends* had its finger on the turbulent pulse of America towards the end of the Sixties. As a record, it still stands up remarkably well after nearly 15 years, not only in the content of the songs, but also in the production techniques.

As Judith Piepe so acutely observed about that album: "It was the first time Paul could use the studio like a guitar." In conjunction with their brilliant producer Roy Halee (who acted as a sort of equivalent to the Beatles' George Martin) the first side of the album is a suite which traces life from the exultation of youth, in *Save The Life Of My Child*, to the resigned melancholy of old age in *Old Friends*. A scrupulous writer, Simon crafted his songs to his and Garfunkel's high standards, consequentially side two of *Bookends* is made up of their four most recent singles, with only one new song, *Punky's Dilemma*. It's a song which finds Simon casting a caustic eye over the

Anne Bancroft as *Mrs. Robinson* with Dustin Hoffman as Benjamin in **The Graduate**

ANDRE CSILLAG

ANDRE CSILLAG

54

superficiality of Californian values, though its tune is lightweight in the *Feelin' Groovy* vein (I'm surprised Simon didn't add a "more intellectual" title in parentheses). And is it only coincidence that the only lady's name in the song is "Maryjane", a synonym for the evil marijuana?

Fakin' It, trivia freaks may care to note, features the voice of Beverley Martyn (once married to the excellent British singer John Martyn, and featured on the sleeve of Bert Jansch's *It Don't Bother Me*). She intones "Good morning Mr Leitch, have you had a busy day?" The Mr Leitch was Donovan, who was a friend of Beverley's. Simon attributed the song to "some hashish reverie." He told Rolling Stone in 1972: "I was thinking to myself 'I'm in a really weird position. I earn my living by writing songs and singing songs . . . If I were born a hundred years ago I wouldn't even be in this country. I'd probably be in Vienna, or wherever my ancestors came from . . . and I wouldn't be a guitarist-songwriter . . . Well what would a Jewish guy be? A tailor.'" Later he talked about his grandfather, who was also called Paul Simon, and had been a tailor in Vienna!

The second side of *Bookends* also marked the first full appearance of *Mrs Robinson* on an S&G album. Although credited as "From the motion picture **The Graduate**", the finished song bears little relation to the one in the film. One can only imagine it's set inside the grounds of a rich asylum where Anne Bancroft's character has gone after the film's conclusion. The "coo coo ca-choo" refrain stretches right back to "Whoo bop a loo chi bop" from *Hey School Girl*.

The song broadens out in the last verse, with Simon plaintively inquiring "Where have you gone Joe DiMaggio/A nation turns its lonely eyes to you." DiMaggio was America's great baseball hero, a legend on the diamond, who later married Marilyn Monroe. A marriage made in Heaven but ending in the divorce courts. It's the baseball loving Paul Simon speaking for the youth of a nation, desperate for a hero on that scale, someone that everyone could admire, a unifying figure for a nation growing further apart. But "Joltin' Joe has left and gone away". The nation mourns, and separates in its search for alternate heroes.

Simon was justifiably proud of the song "(It) was the first time that Jesus was mentioned in a popular song . . . People thought that it was a word you couldn't say in pop music. On the radio they wouldn't play it; they'd find it blasphemous." The song eventually went on to win a Grammy for 'Best Single' of 1968. Garfunkel went and accepted the award on Simon's behalf, who was pleasantly surprised by the accolade: "I didn't expect it. I thought *Hey Jude* was the record of the year." *Mrs Robinson* was bombastically covered by Frank Sinatra (although S&G's arrangement of the song on the 1982 Reunion album was similarly unsubtle). Simon was far happier with Booker T and the MGs version: "They do a great job, very, very funky."

The use of the studio, the willingness to experiment, means that *Bookends* is rich in sounds. The tranquil, acoustic theme which opens the album is swiftly followed by the electronic chaos of *Save The Life Of My Child*, a song about the youth of America, coming out from the dreamy idealism of the hippies. The four verses are succinct and cinematic, with Simon getting a perspective on the song others would ignore. In this case it's the "desperate mother", who provides the chorus and the final, puzzled lines: "What's become of the children/ People asking each other." A sentiment which echoed around America during 1968. The police are disinterested but the media revel in the event "Thought it never made the New York Times/In the Daily News the caption read 'Save the life of my child . . .'" Superb. The multi-tracked vocals sound like the phantoms from a Bosch painting given voice. The opening lines of *Sounds Of Silence* are buried in the mix, recalling Lennon's use of *She Loves You* at the end of *All You Need Is Love* the previous year. In Simon and Garfunkel's case, perhaps they were having a dig at Tom Wilson's electric re-working of their early song. It's an audacious opening to an album, which simply improves as it progresses.

America was another Simon song which touched a nerve in the country. Curiously, for one of Simon and Garfunkel's most popular songs, it's in blank verse, rarely a popular form. The song's seeds apparently lay in a lengthy cross country journey Simon undertook with the inspirational Kathy. The dreamy, wordless voices which usher in the song mark the mellowness which follows the craziness of *Save The Life Of My Child*. The song conjures up visions of **The Graduate** and one can just imagine Dustin Hoffman and Katherine Ross playing the lovers on the Greyhound. The song's climax comes as Simon stares from the window of the bus, "empty and aching" and not knowing why. There are numerous other cars on the turnpike, all out searching for a country, for an identity that's missing, without them realising it. The New Jersey Turnpike is where searches are begun. It also marks the spot where they can come to an end.

Overs are the lovers ten years on, their search ended in a stale, empty marriage. (Zig Zag made a great point that that was Simon blowing a joint just before the song begins, which would fit in perfectly with that sense of disillusion which the song evokes.) The song's most telling line is the laconic "We're just a habit, like saccha-rin." And how many other empty marriages could be summed up by that one line? The couple are condemned to the marriage, like a jail sentence. Each time one partner leaves, they have to stop and think it over. That pause for thought is their failure, their sentence, which will never be commuted.

Voices Of Old People is Garfunkel's most obvious contribution to the album. It's a discomforting intrusion into Simon's seamless suite. Real voices on a collection of songs invariably spoils the fluency. Simon beautifully wraps up the collection with the touching *Old Friends*. Gently beginning with that sublime image of "Old friends, sat on their park bench like bookends," the song builds – with the help of Jimmy Haskell's impressive arrangement – through a series of graphic, poetic images. ("The sounds of the city, *sifting* through trees . . .", the round-toed old men *lost* in their overcoats.) The song arrives inevitably, resignedly "How terribly strange to be 70." Simon sympathetically and deftly portrays the weary strangeness of old age. It's that sense of resignation, of acceptance, that adds extra poignancy to *Old Friends*, with that beautifully sung, lilting "Time it was, and what time it was . . ."

In the end, you're simply left with memories, and a fading, sepia photograph of what was. Like the photograph on the cover, of two young men at the peak of their creativity, shot by Richard Avedon. Garfunkel hovers in the blurred background, while Simon stares

59

straight into the camera, his eyes almost transluscent, like the Star Child of Kubrick's 2001. In time, they will stare at that photograph, when they have grown old, and they will see their youth staring back. When they were young, and the future was theirs for the asking.

Lyrically, Simon was sufficiently proud of the songs to include them on the album's sleeve. The eighteen months had been well spent, even if, in truth, *Bookends* was only half an album, but then Simon was never one to be rushed. Deadlines were anathema to him.

June 1968 saw Simon and Garfunkel occupying the top three positions on the Billboard album chart, while *Mrs Robinson* held sway as the number one single. Simon was swamped with offers for film scores following the success of **The Graduate**, predictably they dwelt on the traumas of youth and the inability of generations to communicate. Simon refused them all, he even turned down **Midnight Cowboy**, because, as he dryly remarked, "I didn't want to look like Dustin Hoffman's songwriter." There were elements of **Midnight Cowboy** on *Bridge Over Troubled Water*, the back cover picture has Simon shuffling after Garfunkel, like Hoffman after Jon Voight. Even on *Keep The Customer Satisfied*, Simon is determined "to keep one step ahead of the shoeshine", in the film, Hoffman's father was a shoeshine.

Spencer Leigh noted a fascinating film project which Simon was allegedly keen on around this time, Franco Zeffirelli's film of St Francis, **Brother Sun And Sister Moon**. It would have offered Simon the opportunity to work with Leonard Bernstein but Zeffirelli couldn't raise the necessary backing and the project lay fallow until 1972, when it was released with music by Donovan Leitch. (Simon is alleged to have contributed to Leonard Bernstein's ambitious *Mass* in 1972.)

Meanwhile, in 1968, Simon was toying with ideas for songs, some of which would not surface for many years. He was rumoured to be the "John Simon" responsible for the Manfred Mann song *My Name Is Jack*, and there was a certain Paul Simon touch to a line about "the Greta Garbo Home for wayward boys and girls." But there actually *was* a John Simon. Paul Simon made one of his few guest appearances on the 1968 *Live Adventures Of Mike Bloomfield And Al Kooper* album. Both were Dylan sidemen of some standing and, according to Kooper, Simon heard the tapes of their version of *Feelin' Groovy*, recorded live at the Fillmore and came in to sing harmony on the last verse when Kooper was mixing the album. (Dylan is alleged to appear on the same album, under the pseudonym 'Roosevelt Gook', playing piano on one track. If this is the case, it marks the only time that Simon and Dylan appeared on a non-compilation album.)

Towards the end of the year, Simon and Garfunkel played a concert for Peace Candidates at Shea Stadium along with Creedence Clearwater Revival, Janis Joplin and John Sebastian. The show raised over 100,000 dollars for Eugene McCarthy, which still didn't stop Richard Nixon being elected in November. December saw Simon complete a song he had begun work on that summer. A work which, I feel, marks Simon and Garfunkel's finest hour – *The Boxer*.

From the gentle acoustic opening to the dramatic orchestral climax five minutes later, *The Boxer* bore all the hallmarks of a classic pop song. Simon, Garfunkel and Halee managed to conjure up Phil Spector's Wall of Sound and blended it with Simon's detailed and touching narrative of the boxer himself. Simon told the NME's Richard Green in May 1969: "It was an experiment. We wanted to record a Christmas album in a church, so we went into one to get the feel and to listen to the sound of the acoustics . . . It was recorded all over the place – the basic tracks in Nashville, the end voices in New York St Paul's (!) Church, the strings in New York Columbia Studios, and the voices there too, and the horns in the church." They worked on a 16 track board, which were really two of CBS's eight tracks linked simultaneously. Simon denied that it took over one hundred hours to record but the effort which went into creating *The Boxer* was obviously painstaking. Out of all of Simon's songs, it is the one which reminds me most of the adage about the sculptor and his statue; that inside every block of stone is a statue waiting to get out. With *The Boxer*, Simon and Garfunkel had created a yardstick by which all their future achievements would be measured.

Much speculation went into the identity of *The Boxer* and many felt it was Simon's most autobiographical song. Others interpreted it as a sustained attack on Dylan. John Bauldie, in the Dylan fanzine **Endless Road**, makes a strong case for the latter. Bauldie cites a revealing quote from Ramblin' Jack Elliott about the young Dylan, scuffing round New York in his early days: "He was very quick, very sarcastic, dealt with people like a boxer, parrying blows and remarks, and skipping out in a hurry." The song is interpreted as a put down of Dylan's insistence at disguising his comfortable middle class background; of shedding Robert Zimmerman in the process of inventing Bob Dylan ("Lie la lie").

It does fit into the scheme of Simon's song, even down to the cautionary "Come on from the whores on 7th Avenue" – the old CBS offices used to be on 7th Avenue. But Simon also had elements of that ability to shed his past, as we have seen, he was able to gloss over the Tom and Jerry days, and when Bob Shelton interviewed the duo for his New York Times profile, neither of them even mentioned their teenage career.

But it would be petty to see Simon's masterpiece simply as a veiled attack on Dylan. The lyric was his best to date, a beautifully concise narrative with elements of the young Hemingway and Kerouac sewn in. It's ultimately a song of optimism, but an optimism forged in the harshness of reality. The "poor boy" in the song punches through life, constantly put down and harried, arriving at the bitter realisation that "A man hears what he wants to hear/And disregards the rest." The final verse succinctly paints a picture of a young man, a boxer, standing alone in a clearing, with only his scars and punch-drunk memories. It's a mixture of frustration, humility and dignity that causes him to cry "I am leaving, I am leaving/But the fighter still remains." What remains is that essential something that cannot be crushed, that spark of decency, of dignity, which will sustain him through the bleak future. The song really came alive when it was made available in stereo on the *Bridge* album, the thumping sax underpinning the narrative, the flawless horn solo and culminating in the epic orchestral fade with that final long glorious chorus of "Lie la lie", until it comes round full circle, tailing off with an acoustic guitar.

It was Simon and Garfunkel's only record of 1969. It was enough and, as a foretaste of their next album, it was beguiling.

Following his involvement with Mike Nichols in **The Graduate**,

Art Garfunkel eagerly accepted a role in his next film, and began shooting **Catch 22** in January 1969. Garfunkel saw the role not only as an opportunity to pursue his acting career but also as a chance to escape the rigours of the mixing of the next S&G album. The role of Captain Nately was considerable but Garfunkel anticipated finishing the film by June. However, the location work in Mexico and Italy over-ran its schedule with no end in sight. With Garfunkel committed to Nichols film, Simon and Garfunkel's immediate plans were held in abeyance.

Joseph Heller's novel was probably the screen 'catch' of the decade. Few titles have entered the language as quickly as **Catch 22**. The novel was a classic black comedy of men and war, and Garfunkel's role was as the film's innocent, adrift in a world of corruption. **Catch 22** was a big budget, star-studded film, including Orson Welles, who had bought the rights to the book soon after publication but could never raise the backing. Paul Simon was to have played Dunbar in the film, but translating a 300 page novel into a two hour film meant certain incidents and characters had to be eliminated, and Dunbar was one of them.

Simon was married in the summer of 1969, and his wife Peggy replaced the enigmatic Kathy as his muse. The time had come to prepare for the next Simon and Garfunkel album. Simon wrote the bulk of the songs towards the end of 1969 and early 1970 for their next release – *Bridge Over Troubled Water*.

Artie as Captain Nately in
Catch 22

Chapter Five

Quoted in Presidential campaigns, heard at christenings and funerals, in supermarkets and cabarets all over the world. Everywhere there's a record player, it's odds on that CBS 63699 has been there too. From the day of its release, *Bridge Over Troubled Water* was regarded as a classic. But the problems of its creation and release were manifold: Garfunkel was marooned in Mexico on **Catch 22**; months of actual recording, Simon unhappy at Garfunkel's penchant for sweetness, coupled with the duo's sense of growing apart.

John Hammond, the man at CBS responsible for discovering Aretha Franklin, Bob Dylan and Bruce Springsteen, remembers Simon and Garfunkel linking up the company's two 16 track machines to create an unheard of 32 tracks to record the album which he believes took then eight hundred hours of studio time. It had been eighteen months since the release of *Bookends*, and Simon later recalled that Garfunkel's involvement with **Catch 22** was a contributory factor. Neither Simon or Garfunkel could decide on what the single should be, they felt that a rocky number like *Cecilia* stood more chance of picking up airplay. CBS's Clive Davis remembered going to hear the finished tapes of the album for the first time in the studio, along with Paul's parents and his brother Eddie. Davis immediately suggested the album's title track should be the single: "I can't be absolutely positive, but this is one time to go for a home run. It is the age of rock and this is a ballad – and a long one at that – but *if* it hits, it could become a classic."

Hindsight, of course, reveals Davis to have been absolutely right. To date, *Bridge Over Troubled Water* has sold somewhere in the region of 11 million albums world-wide. It collected more Grammy awards than any other album in rock history. It was the first single and album to simultaneously top the British and American charts. It stayed on the British album charts longer than any other rock album. Statistically, it's in a class of its own, what is fascinating is *why*. It is by no means Simon and Garfunkel's best album, yet it was the one that reached far beyond their normal audience, and kept statisticians and CBS happy for years.

Simon and Garfunkel were as surprised as anyone at the album's enormous success, they were obviously pleased with the finished product, but then, they always set themselves the task of improving on their previous album. It was the title track that drew people by the million to the album. The genesis of *Bridge Over Troubled Water* lay in gospel, a type of music which fascinated Simon. Bob Shelton of the New York Times remembered a gospel song Roberta Flack recalled from her schooldays called *Don't Trouble The Water*, which he was sure Simon knew. Simon himself told Chris Charlesworth that it was the Reverend Claude Juter (formerly of the gospel group the Swan Silvertones) that was the real influence behind the song: "Had it not been for him, I would never have written *Bridge Over Troubled Water* . . . He recorded a song called *Oh Mary Don't You Weep*. The guy has probably the best falsetto voice in the world, and somewhere in the middle he scat sings 'I'll be your bridge over deep water if you trust in my name' . . . I was working on this tune at the time. There was no lyric, it was called 'Hymn', and really, that's how it came about."

Simon later repaid his debt to the Rev. Juter, when the latter sang on *Take Me To The Mardi Gras* from Simon's second solo album in 1973. When recording the song, Simon instructed pianist Larry Knechtel to "play gospel". Simon also revealed that when the strings were being scored for the final verse, the arranger mis-heard Garfunkel's singing, and the original string part – which Simon has framed – is titled *Like A Pitcher Of Water*!

A number of people commented on the similarities between *Bridge* and the Beatles *Let It Be*, which were released around the same time. Simon told Rolling Stone: "They are very similar songs . . . sort of in their general musical feel, and lyrically. They're sort of both hopeful songs and resting, peaceful songs . . . it's one of those weird things, and it happened simultaneously." That sense of tranquility on *Bridge* is perfectly rendered by Garfunkel's flawless vocal and the song evokes a sense of serenity. By the final verse, there's a sense of determination. It was that final verse which caused quite a controversy at the time, many people interpreted the "sail on silvergirl" line as a reference to a hypodermic needle, and the whole song was seen as a hymn to drugs! The point was eventually clarified when it was learnt that Simon wrote the song specifically for his wife Peggy, who was prematurely grey. (Even as late as 1982, a trio of pastors condemned Simon and Garfunkel's records for promoting drugs.)

In retrospect, it is easy to see various clues on the album which point towards a permanent split in the partnership. *The Only Living Boy In New York* finds Simon alone, bidding Artie farewell. In the song, Garfunkel reverts to his earlier rock persona (the Tom in Tom and Jerry) as Simon wishes him good luck in **Catch 22**: "Tom, get your plane right on time/I know your part'll go fine/Fly down to Mexico . . ."

And at the end of *So Long, Frank Lloyd Wright*, buried down in the mix, while Garfunkel sings "So long, so long", you can hear Simon say "So long already, Artie."

El Condor Pasa came from a Los Incas album, which Simon had been given by the group when he played a gig with them in Paris in 1965. He added his own (albeit mediocre) lyrics to the traditional Peruvian melody, and got Los Incas in to record the song with him. It's an early example of Simon's ability at assimilating diverse musical influences. He told Chris Charlesworth later: "I like to play with a lot of musicians that are outside the sphere of rock 'n' roll . . . I find the experience to be socially enjoyable too, they turn out to be nice people . . ."

Cecilia Simon called "a little piece of magical fluff", which came

about from laying down a simple percussive rhythm track, with simple guitar phrases and Simon singing the first lines that came into his head. *Keep The Customer Satisfied* is a brassy, rocking number, the all too rare sound of Simon and Garfunkel letting their hair down. There's a typically audacious Simon rhyme in "I get slandered, libelled/I hear words I never heard in the Bible," which tells you a lot about the boy on the run in the song, and his background.

So Long, Frank Lloyd Wright apparently came about after Garfunkel, who was fascinated by architecture, jokingly suggested that Simon couldn't write a song about that influential architect who had died in 1959. *Baby Driver* had been the B-side of *The Boxer* the previous year, a tongue in cheek, autobiographical song. As mentioned earlier, Simon's father was "the family bassman" but whether he was "a prominent frogman" during the war is unknown. Who cares? It is a lovely line.

Simon was unhappy with *Why Don't You Write Me?* realising that to get that authentic, shuffling ska rhythm he'd intended, he'd have to go to Jamaica. *Bye Bye Love* is, of course, the old Everly Brothers hit, Tom and Jerry's homage to their early idols. Simon and Garfunkel had been recording a number of shows from their recent tours for a possible live album, and both were particularly fascinated by the audience handclapping from this number in Ames, Iowa. It was the only official live Simon and Garfunkel track to be issued during their career together, and offers the rare opportunity to hear them working with a full band live.

Song For The Asking was written early in 1970, and sounds like a valediction. It's Simon alone, almost begging not to be taken too seriously ("Ask me and I will play/So sweetly I'll make you smile"). Maybe that's part of the album's global success, that it presented a less earnest Simon and Garfunkel, with catchy, rocky little songs like *Cecilia* and *Keep The Customer Satisfied*. On *Song For The Asking*, it's like Simon's shaking off that mantle of intensity he had acquired. It was something both he and Garfunkel were aware of and were keen to name one of their albums *So Young, Yet So Full Of Pain*, as a deliberate joke on their studious image.

It is still difficult though, to reconcile a patchy, at times brilliant, album as one of the best selling albums of all time. Simon told Rolling Stone in 1971: "I certainly don't know why it should have been so much bigger than the others . . . I guess it has a very broad appeal, that's the only reason I can think of. A lot of people who may never have bought albums before, or ever heard of Simon and Garfunkel, got into it." *Bridge* has only been equalled in terms of sales by Simon's old partner, Carole King, with *Tapestry*, Fleetwood Mac's *Rumours* and the soundtrack for **Saturday Night Fever**.

The success of *Bridge Over Troubled Water* meant that any Simon and Garfunkel concert of 1970 was an instant sell out. From being a cult attraction (albeit a large one) they had suddenly crossed into the field of superstardom. June 1970 saw Bob Dylan cover his only Paul Simon song, when he included *The Boxer* on his *Self Portrait* album. It was a pretty ragged effort with no real attempt at synchronising his double-tracked vocals. If Simon's song was a knock at Dylan, then Dylan's rushed reply may well have been his revenge. Simon was suitably diplomatic in his comments: "Like anything Dylan does, it has its own thing. He did it differently, and I don't think anyone could

69

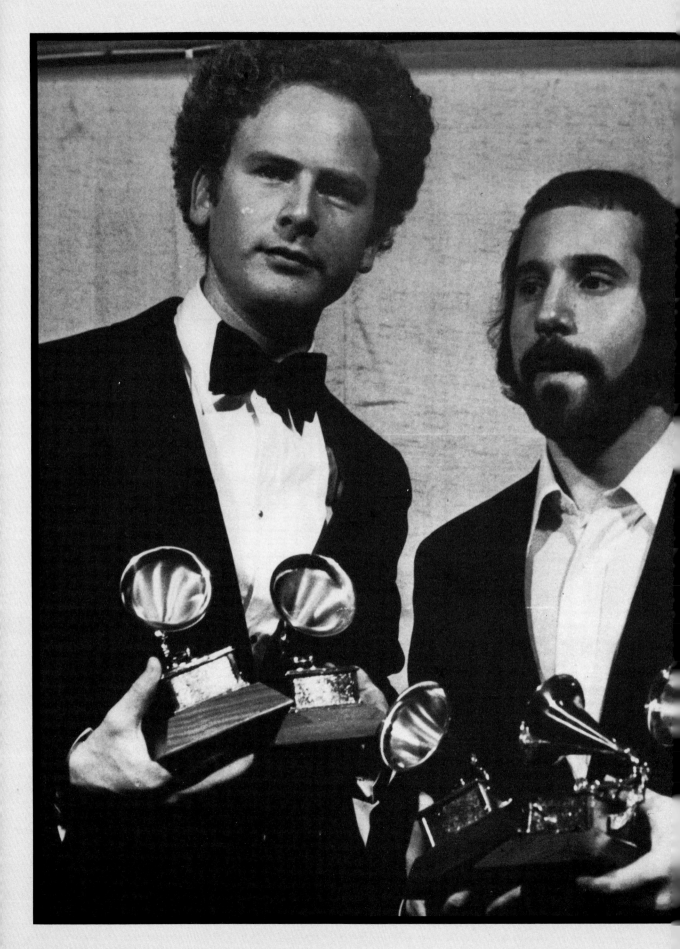

do that. Dylan's version makes me smile." (Unfortunately, Simon's thoughts are not available regarding Emmylou Harris's sensitive rendering on her 1980 *Roses In The Snow* album.)

The wheel also span full circle when Elvis Presley covered *Bridge* that same year. It was Elvis who had set Paul Simon, like so many of his generation, on the rock 'n' roll trail, and here was the man they still called "The King" covering a song by one of his subjects. But Simon, althouth gratified, didn't rate the Elvis version very highly, going into print as preferring Aretha Franklin's.

With the album finished and their touring commitments honoured, their only joint project was a television special. An hour long show, it had been commissioned by the Bell Telephone Company, who saw it as an opportunity to present sixty minutes' worth of S&G singing their best known songs, courtesy of Bell Telephones. Simon and Garfunkel saw it differently and collaborated with actor Charles Grodin (who had worked with Garfunkel on **Catch 22**) to present their view of America at the end of an old decade, and the beginning of a new.

Simon spoke bitterly of the show's problems to Rolling Stone in May 1970: "We decided to do a show on America, instead of just having a show with duets with Glen and the dance number . . . We had a sequence with the two Kennedys and Martin Luther King that was played while we did *Bridge Over Troubled Water*, and they objected to that . . . they said if we showed this film, where you have Jesse Jackson and Ralph Abernathy and Bobby Kennedy in it, if we showed this film in Alabama we will be in tremendous trouble . . ." Bell weren't at all keen on the political elements of the show, they complained of footage of Woodstock, Vietnam, union boycotts, but "could live with the Lone Ranger!"

A great deal of effort went into the show, which was aired only once (in a drastically trimmed version) then forgotten by the company. It was a problem which bothered Simon and Garfunkel. Despite the massive success of *Bridge*, cracks were beginning to appear in the thirteen year old partnership. There were originally to have been twelve songs on the album, Simon had written a vitriolic number called *Cuba Si, Nixon No* which attacked the President's policy which stated that American residents were not allowed to visit Cuba as it was a Communist country. Garfunkel was not keen on the song and refused to sing it. He grudgingly consented but only if the backing was in the style of a Bach chorale which Simon felt was wholly unsuitable. Simon told Jon Landau in 1972: "We were fighting over which was gonna be the twelfth song, and then I said 'Fuck it, put it out with eleven songs, if that's the way it is.' We were at the end of our energies over that."

Both Simon and Garfunkel were approaching 30, they had spent half their lives together as friends and partners, both felt the need to flex their creative muscles apart from each other.

Despite the problems associated with **Catch 22**, and its subsequent mixed reviews, Garfunkel had been fascinated by the process of film making and acting and had eagerly accepted Mike Nichols offer to star in his next film, **Carnal Knowledge**. Simon envisaged a holiday, then cutting a solo album, getting into a funkier style of music, he told Landau: "Artie's taste is much more to the sweet . . . sweet and big and lush. There's nothing wrong with that, there's a place for lush-

71

ness. It's not generally the way I go." It was the perennial problem of "musical differences" which played a part in the subsequent split. As composer, singer and arranger of the most successful album in rock history, the pressure was obviously on Simon to top it. He saw his continuing partnership with Garfunkel taking him further into musical areas he wished to avoid. Garfunkel's penchant for lush ballads, which ideally suited his voice, were not the direction Simon saw his music going.

There was never any real announcement that Simon and Garfunkel had split. Their final concert together, in the summer of 1970, had taken them home to Forest Hills, where they finished with the Crew Cuts' *Earth Angel*. Everyone was eager to see how they could top *Bridge Over Troubled Water*, and that sort of pressure weighed heavily on Simon. There had been a tacit agreement that Garfunkel would go off to film with Mike Nichols and that Simon would prepare a solo album, the two just drifted apart, rather than finally severing the link. Chris Charlesworth asked Simon in 1975 that even if *Bridge* hadn't been the total success it automatically had been, would they still have split? "Yes. I think that almost all partnerships break up. It's an inevitable by-product of the growth. Really, Artie and I have quite different musical tastes. His albums are quite different from mine . . . I think we would have come into conflict anyway."

Obviously, as composer, the creative impetus of the partnership came from Paul Simon. Garfunkel's actual contribution to the partnership has frequently been questioned. Garfunkel, though, always seemed to favour the softer option – his arrangement of *Benedictus*, the wistful singing on *For Emily* . . ., the lead on *Bridge*, but it was, inevitably, a minor role. As creator of the songs, Simon played the largest creative role. Garfunkel's part came into evidence when it came to the arrangement and production of Simon's songs. Simon told Rolling Stone soon after *Bridge* was released: "Artie's there from the earliest . . . He has the ears that are listening inside." But two years later, with the partnership rent asunder, Simon was telling the same magazine: "Musically, it was not a creative team, too much, because Artie is a singer and I'm a writer and player and a singer. We didn't work together on a creative level and prepare the songs. I did that."

Simon did stress, though, that working on an S&G album with such a creative producer as Roy Halee was very much a three way partnership: "Each person had a relatively equal say. So, in other words, if Roy and Artie said 'Let's do a long ending on *The Boxer*, I said 'Two out of three' and did it their way. I didn't say 'Hey, this is my song, I don't want to do it like that.'" Roy Halee had been a young engineer at the CBS studios in New York and had first worked with the duo under Tom Wilson on their first *Wednesday Morning* album, but gradually became more involved on the production side as Simon and Garfunkel became disillusioned with their "official" producer Bob Johnston (who also numbered Bob Dylan, Leonard Cohen and Johnny Cash among his charges). Simon once spoke to Lon Goddard, then at CBS, of Johnston's role: "As a producer? Johnston was only there to find out who wanted a chicken salad sandwich!"

Garfunkel spoke to Chris Charlesworth in 1975 about Roy Halee: "Roy comes out of the Masterworks department of Columbia

Records, so he's an engineer and particularly a sound man. He's very conservative . . . " From another 1975 interview, Garfunkel spoke of the partnership: "There were songs on our albums that I, as an individual, didn't identify with at all. Actually, I would have liked to have done much more of the singing. I always thought that I was by far the better singer of the two of us." It was something that Simon was aware of, he told Jon Landau: "Many times on stage, when I'd be sitting off to the side and Larry Knechtel would be playing the piano and Artie would be singing *Bridge*, people would stamp and cheer when it was over. And I would think 'That's my song, man. Thank you very much, I wrote that song.'" It's not as self-centred as it sounds, many people still think that Simon and Garfunkel's songs were written by the duo.

Simon and Garfunkel's fifteen year career lasted a lot longer than many marriages. From the teenage success of *Hey School Girl* to the massive global appeal of *Bridge Over Troubled Water*, they had achieved everything they could have wished for. Simon's songs had acutely monitored society's changes, growing in structure from his simple, alienated works to complex narrative. He was capable of writing haunting love songs like *For Emily* . . . as well as sweeping stories like *The Boxer*. With Garfunkel's flawless harmonising and the duo's insistence on studio perfection, their audience grew and grew.

Their years as Simon and Garfunkel had met with a critical and commercial success beyond the dreams of their contemporaries. Contemporaries like Phil Ochs, who doggedly clung to the belief that his songs were a weapon. Like Dylan, forging wayward paths for others to follow, but frequently tripping up in his trail-blazing efforts.

Simon and Garfunkel proved there was a vast audience prepared to listen to brilliantly constructed pop songs with intelligent lyrics. Their appeal ran the gamut from cynical rock critics to fans who rarely bought any other records. Not everyone succumbed though. Bob Shelton was struck "by a kind of Mickey Mouse, timid, contrived side" in Simon's writing. "Through Dylan, Van Ronk, all of those guys, what was really being venerated was . . . a rough, ethnic natural, dirty sound . . . They were sounding very suburban . . . I can admire the skill, the craft, the polish . . . I would not rank (Simon) among important rock poets. I would rank him among skilful rock lyric versifiers."

Bob Woffinden, in the NME Encyclopedia of Rock, was equally harsh: "The key to Simon and Garfunkel's success was probably that they offered safe, synthetic protest; they questioned society's values without challenging them . . . Essentially, they were all-American boys; with their lavish, wide-screen production jobs, theirs was the ultimate coffee table music."

There are elements of truth in both criticisms, but I feel Simon's abilities as a rock lyricist have been seriously underrated. He helped bring a poetic discipline to rock, never afraid to hone the words into perfect shape over lengthy periods. Simon experimented with blank verse, unusual verse and chorus structures, shaping and perfecting them like talented songsmiths from earlier generations. Paul Simon probably has as much in common with Cole Porter as he has with Bob Dylan. Yet rarely have his lyrics been accorded the acclaim attached to Dylan or John Lennon. There was a fascinating exposition on

Simon's craft by Mike Davies in a 1976 issue of *Nuggets*, but Simon seems to have fallen prey to the intellectual snobbery which cannot allow that anything successful can have any redeeming intellectual merit.

Simon's output has been remarkably small, considering he's been writing songs for the best part of quarter of a century. It is a tribute, then, to the quality of those songs that so many of them have become classics. The universality of Simon's themes evoke a strong response in audiences across the world, they feel they can identify strongly with the characters and situations he so scrupulously depicts. Whether it's the child-like sincerity of a love song, like *Kathy's Song* or the sheer exuberance of *Feelin' Groovy*. Whether it's a hymn to alienation like *The Sounds Of Silence* or the personal poignancy of *Leaves That Are Green*, Simon's songs touched the hearts and minds of many people during Simon and Garfunkel's career.

With the Sixties barely behind them, Simon and Garfunkel's parting swiftly followed that of the Beatles. Dylan's *Self Portrait* and *New Morning* albums seemed as though his finest hour had passed. The first year of a new decade seemed to mark the end of an era.

Chapter Six

America during the early 1970s was a confused and confusing place. The initial fervour of the youth rebellion of the late Sixties had died bloodily on the campus of Kent State when four students were shot by National Guardsmen. The Vietnam war was spreading silently across the border into Cambodia. The idyllic world of open air festivals reached a fatal nemesis at Altamount in December 1969, when a young black was murdered by the Hell's Angels in front of 300,000 Rolling Stones fans. The devout naivety of rock music was gradually replaced by an insipid mellowness. Denim fans now paid homage at the court of King James (Taylor) and Queen Carole (King). Rock music was moving towards spectacle. As bands grew bigger and bigger, so did the venues. Dylan remained silent for three years; Lennon was purging himself of the Beatle experience by releasing the harrowing *Plastic Ono Band* album in 1970. The mood was switching towards acquiescence rather than rebellion in the music.

Simon postponed the pressure in topping *Bridge Over Troubled Water*. It was to be two years before his first solo album hit the racks. Garfunkel was busy filming **Carnal Knowledge**, and waited three years before unleashing his solo debut. One thing neither Simon or Garfunkel were in a hurry to resume was live work, both saw it as a necessary obligation. Usually they performed alone, just the two of them accompanied by Simon's guitar. Latterly, pianist Larry Knechtel would join Garfunkel onstage for *Bridge*. They did try some dates with a full live band, but audiences were disappointed, they just wanted Simon and Garfunkel, singing their best known songs.

The choice of material for their set was a perennial dilemma. They were under a certain obligation to their audience to play the songs *they* had paid to hear, but were equally keen to incorporate new material. Simon expounded on this theme to Rolling Stone in 1970: "You know, it gets very hard singing *The Sounds Of Silence*, as you can imagine . . . People want to hear the songs you're famous for. I was talking to Dylan, and said that's my problem with going out on the road. It gets boring for me because of this. They want to hear *The Sounds Of Silence*. He said 'Well, I'd like to see you, and if I came to see you I'd want to see you sing *The Sounds Of Silence* and *Scarborough Fair*.' When I saw the Rolling Stones, and they played *Satisfaction*, I said 'That's the Rolling Stones playing *Satisfaction*. That song I know well by the Rolling Stones, there they are doing it.' I don't care whether they did it good or bad or anything . . . So I think it's very hard to ever escape from that."

KOBAL

Life on the road held little appeal for Simon and Garfunkel, even such permanent attractions as groupies hardly featured. According to Simon: "Simon and Garfunkel had a peculiar type of groupies, we had the poetic groupies. The girls that followed us around weren't necessarily looking to sleep with us, as much as they were looking to read their poetry or discuss literature . . . I wasn't into picking up girls on the road. Couldn't do it. Too embarrassing for me. I wasn't interested in their poetry either!" The curious, unnatural life of a rock musician on the road was something which Simon fully explored in his film of **One Trick Pony** later on.

There was always the temporary abandonment which drugs offered. Smoking dope was something Simon was into when playing the folk clubs in England years before.

Both Simon and Garfunkel dropped acid, with varying results. Simon eventually gave up drugs and cigarettes when he entered

Jack Nicholson (left) and Arthur Garfunkel in **Carnal Knowledge**

analysis. Like many of his talented contemporaries, Paul Simon found success brought a peculiar type of pressure to bear on him. Judith Piepe has kept in touch with Simon regularly since the days he used to crash at her flat, and I asked her if she thought Simon was happy with the success that had come so suddenly to him? Whether the attendant uncertainties, such as phsychiatry, weren't a sad reflection on that price of success? "English people go to the dentist. Americans have analysis. English women talk to their hairdresser, English men talk to the barman. New York Americans talk to their analyst."

Carnal Knowledge was released in 1971, starring Jack Nicholson and *Arthur* Garfunkel. Jules Feiffer's script chronicled the sexual adventures of two characters, from college days to middle age. It was critically better received than **Catch 22**, and Garfunkel's performance certainly stood up next to such seasoned professionals as Jack Nicholson and Ann Margaret. It was a confident performance and one which indicated that Garfunkel had a promising career ahead of him in film. But he waited nearly a decade before returning to the screen and, since he can't have been short of offers, it was presumably because he is as scrupulous about his choice of his film roles as he was about his music.

Simon returned, briefly, to live work in August 1971, at a fund raising concert for Senator George McGovern at Shea Stadium. It was not a happy event, Simon included a couple of familiar S&G songs, and battled with three songs from his forthcoming solo album. But the crowd was restless and was having a running battle with the police throughout the show. Simon appealed, cajoled, for silence, swore at the police, and stormed off halfway through *Scarborough Fair*.

More importantly, Simon started teaching a "Songwriting And Record Making" course at New York University during 1971. Among his pupils were Melissa Manchester and Maggie and Terre Roche, who appeared on his second solo album, before achieving success with their other sister Suzie late in the Seventies as the Roches. Simon admitted he couldn't teach people how to write a song, but "what I can do mainly is tell them what I've learned . . . I like talking about songwriting. I like to hear what people are writing and I'd like to spare people some of the grief that I went through by learning by trial and error." In later years, with a wallful of gold records and Grammies Simon himself undertook a songwriting course.

But all public attention was focused on the first solo albums from Simon and Garfunkel. Simon was first off the mark in February 1972, two years exactly after *Bridge*. His debut solo work was to have been titled *Duncan*, but he eventually settled on the imaginative title of *Paul Simon*. It was recorded over a year at studios in Jamaica, Paris, San Francisco and New York. On first impressions, it was a lot *harder* than an S&G album. Simon was working with basic rhythm sections, and used little colouring in conveying the mood of his new songs. Simon had gone in print as being very impressed by the funky feel of Ry Cooder's first album in 1970. The lush sweetness of S&G he left with Garfunkel, the album was characterised by the quality S&G brought to their recordings but *Paul Simon* sounded a lot freer. Simon was unhappy at the lack of spontaneity working with Garfunkel and Halee and, although his solo album doesn't sound like it was bashed out on a four track before opening time, it is a lot looser and funkier.

Some of the songs had been around for years (*Armistice Day* had been begun in 1968) but most had been written fairly swiftly for the album. The diversity of the musical influences proved that Simon had been busy assimilating different styles of music, as typified by the album's opening track, the reggae *Mother And Child Reunion*. The title came from a chicken and eggs dish which fascinated Simon on a Chinese restaurant menu! From such an unlikely source, Simon wrote a touching and haunting song about the death of a loved one. From the lingering and poignant opening lines "No I would not give you false hope/On this strange and mournful day", the song emphatically marked the return of Paul Simon.

It is important to note that Simon was probably the first major white rock 'n' roll artist to utilise reggae rhythms on record. Up until then, reggae had always been considered an inferior form of music and in England it was characterised as "skinhead music". It was not until the following year, with the release of Bob Marley's *Stir It Up* and Jimmy Cliff's **The Harder They Come** film that reggae was accepted in America (in fact, Rolling Stone in their 1972 Simon interview, were so unfamiliar with the form they consistently refer to it as "regga*l*"!). Simon was determined to get an authentic reggae feel on the track, particularly after the half-hearted effort on *Why Don't You Write Me?*. He told Chris Charlesworth: "I actually came to go down there after hearing a Jimmy Cliff song *Vietnam*. I called the producer, who was called Leslie Kong and said 'I'd like to come to Jamaica and record with those musicians.'" Simon had always been fascinated by the shuffling rhythms of reggae and he fondly remembered Desmond Dekker and Millie Small records from his days in England. His decision to cut *Mother And Child Reunion* at Dynamic Sounds was not without incident. The musicians who played on the record were used to getting ten dollars per song, which could mean 60 dollars a day by their standards. They were distrustful of Simon's technique in recording one song over three or four days, but he eventually renegotiated their contracts to mutual satisfaction.

The album's next song, *Duncan*, showed that Simon had lost none of his narrative flair. Reminiscent of *The Boxer* in structure, the backing was, however, distinctly un-Simon and Garfunkel.

Los Incas was the Peruvian group Simon incorporated on *El Condor Pasa* but here they were allowed to play a fuller role. It was Simon's declared ambition to work with musicians outside the rock 'n' roll sphere and, true to his word, it was happening. Lincoln Duncan is a fisherman's child, "born in the boredom and the chowder" of the Canadian Maritimes, the loneliness of his early life is succinctly summed up with the observation that "these motel walls are cheap". In just a few lines, Simon sketches Duncan's background: "My father was a fisherman/My mama was a fisherman's friend" brilliantly conveys his home life. His loneliness is shared by a bible pusher in a parking lot and is seen as Duncan's salvation. The biblical theme is conjured up towards the end of the song but Simon's last verse is a musician's memory of his seduction: "Even now that sweet memory lingers/I was playing my guitar, lying underneath the stars/Just thanking the Lord for my fingers."

Everything Put Together Falls Apart could well be Simon's commentary on Simon and Garfunkel and it's been suggested that the reason he wrote the song was to include "Paraphenalia" in the first

Paul Simon in 1972

line. *Run That Body Down* is a poor song, one idea, one tune, stretched over four minutes. Paul and Peggy Simon are worried about their health, Paul then asks us to worry about our bodily abuse. Simon himself was particularly pleased with *Armistice Day*, particularly the opening lines, which he felt were technically adept. That first verse does have a lovely *sound* to it, particularly a line like "Shufflin' brown tunes", which recalls a feeling, like "dappled and drowsy" from *Feelin' Groovy*. It's not a particularly distinguished song, and falls apart after its gentle, acoustic opening, and can best be summed up by the chorus "Armistice Day, Armistice Day/That's all I really wanted to say."

Me And Julio Down By The Schoolyard is a knockout little pop song which came about from a tape loop Simon had been toying with. Lyrically, he admitted, he had no idea just what "the mama saw" that was against the law! It's an effervescent delight, a song for sunny summer days, but what seems like its lyrical flippancy, does have a sort of topical seriousness. The "radical priest" mentioned in the final verse was probably Father Daniel Berrigan, an outspoken priest who could not tolerate the church's indifference to the Vietnam war, and was militant in his opposition to it.

Peace Like A River sounds like an S&G song, recalling *The Only Living Boy In New York*, with its massed choirs of multi-tracked Simons. Now it could be seen as a trailer for *American Tune* of the following year, with Simon musing on the parlous times the country was going through. I believe the song is connected with the 1968 riots at the Democratic Convention in Chicago, and the subsequent trial of 'The Chicago Seven', when black activist Bobby Seale was bound and gagged during the 'democratic' trial. There are also elements of Dylan's 1964 *Chimes Of Freedom*, notably the "starry-eyed" line.

Papa Hobo is another song for the individual, the roamer, in this case one who will not succumb to Detroit's "automotive dream". It's an elusive, fragmentary song, but nonetheless charming. "Carbon and monoxide/That ole Detroit perfume" are two telling lines, that successfully capture the time and the place in so few words, but then, after all, that is part of the poet's craft. *Hobo's Blues* deliberately follows *Papa Hobo*, but here we find Simon (if you'll pardon the pun) playing second fiddle to the world's greatest jazz violinist. Stephane Grappelli achieved immortality when he played with the legendary gypsy guitarist Django Rheinhardt in Paris in the Thirties. Simon here is quite happy to strum alongside Grappelli.

How determined Simon was to record with Grappelli is uncertain, he also approached Fairport Convention's Dave Swarbrick to play fiddle on the track but then changed his mind. *Hobo's Blues* strikes me as an almost desperate attempt by Simon to prove how versatile he was on his first solo album, incorporating jazz, as well as reggae, blues and South American music into his style.

Paranoia Blues features one of the foremost exponents of bottleneck guitar, Stefan Grossman. It was rumoured at one time that Simon and Grossman would be forming a full time partnership but this is the only available track of them together. Grossman later went on to found the excellent Kicking Mule Records which highlighted many new guitarists.) Lyrically, *Paranoia Blues* finds Simon back in the Chinese restaurant that inspired *Mother And Child Reunion*. Simon has frequently professed his love for New York, but here he gets "the paranoia blues/From knockin' around in New York City." Maybe it's the theft of his "Lin Chow Fon" that so upsets him!

Congratulations nearly wraps up the proceedings. Borrowing from Little Anthony and the Imperials *Tears On My Pillow*, it's a lengthy flowing ballad, which relies on Larry Knechtel's keyboards, inevitably drawing comparisons with *Bridge*. Simon's wondering whether a relationship can survive in these troubled times. It's a sustained, heartfelt song which, although concentrating on the problems between two lovers, cannot help but notice the people "waiting in line in the courtrooms today." A subdued, dignified end to an impressive debut album.

Paul Simon had not vanquished the spirit of Simon and Garfunkel with one solo album, he could never expect to do that. Comparisons were inevitably made with his work with Garfunkel, but what *Paul Simon* did prove was that Simon had lost none of his lyrical flair or musical enterprise. With the massive success of *Bridge Over Troubled Water*, Simon was seen by many as a talented artist who had foresaken his artistic credibility for commercial success. The trouble with success on the scale of *Bridge* is that Simon's genuine abilities were overlooked. Sadly, people were probably more familiar with the hundreds of ersatz cover versions, rather than Simon and Garfunkel's epic original.

Paul Simon displayed Simon's credibility was still intact and, although there was nothing on the scale of *The Boxer*, there were plenty of diverse tracks which demonstrated Simon was flexing his creative muscle, rather than lying back and coasting on his past reputation. Perhaps the album's most durable quality is the effort Simon put into its creation. He lavished care and attention on the album, celebrating all manner of musical areas. The most important half of the fabled partnership had proved he had lost none of his inventiveness. Despite the success of *Paul Simon*, there was still an incredible interest in the winning partnership of Simon and Garfunkel.

When a successful act splits up, its record company is rarely slow off the mark to repackage any back product in search of sales but there was really very little CBS could concoct in the case of Simon and Garfunkel. Simon had frequently admitted he never kept any songs 'in the can', as proved by Clive Davis's problems with **The Graduate** soundtrack. CBS weren't idle though. Within months of Simon's solo album, *Simon And Garfunkel's Greatest Hits* was available. Simon's hand was discernible in the compilation for, instead of simply regurgitating familiar S&G songs, previously unavailable live versions of *For Emily . . .*, *Feelin' Groovy*, *Homeward Bound* and *Kathy's Song* were included.

The obvious move would have been a complete 'live' Simon and Garfunkel album. CBS had recorded many of their gigs with that idea in mind, and a concert at Tufts University in 1966 apparently got as far as acetate form before it was quashed. It's a shame it never made it onto record. Apart from live versions of familiar songs like *Homeward Bound* and *I Am A Rock*, it also offers the opportunity to hear songs like *Dangling Conversation* and *Poem On The Underground Wall* stripped of their studio wizardry and marvel at S&G's ability at reproducing them. The Tufts' show contains a lot of interesting dialogue between the songs, Simon reminiscing about his 'cool' image and the circumstances surrounding *Feelin' Groovy*; Garfunkel

Art Garfunkel in 1972

speaks of *Benedictus* and the problems getting the *Wednesday Morning* cover shot. There's also a version of the otherwise un-available *Red Rubber Ball*.

Simon and Garfunkel though, really did have a remarkably small repertoire. The basis of their live performances was still, basically, the songs from *The Paul Simon Songbook*, with updates from their current album. In concert, they did feature covers of other songs, like the Everly Brothers' *Lightning Express*, or Gene Autry's 1931 hit *That Silver Haired Daddy Of Mine*. It was not until 1982 that the world got to hear an official live S&G album but *The Concert In Central Park* was as much an event as a live album.

Simon and Garfunkel were, of course, bootlegged. It was almost a

testimony to an artist's status, how many bootlegs were available in their name. It was a particularly redundant exercise in S&G's case, so much of their songs' strength lay in the attention to detail they paid in the studio, which second or third generation tapes could never reproduce. Various non-concept recordings do exist, but they add little to our knowledge of the duo.

Chez is a tape Simon made up for Kathy in England in 1965, mainly guitar instrumentals or versions of songs featured on the *Songbook*. There is also a tape of Art Garfunkel singing alone into a tape recorder in New York in 1963. It features unaccompanied versions of then popular songs, like *You'll Never Walk Alone*, *Sh'boom*, *All I Have To Do Is Dream* and *Devoted To You*, which strengthen the Everly Brothers bond. Garfunkel sounds stilted and uncomfortable, unhappily tackling rock 'n' roll standards.

Even live bootlegs add little lustre to the S&G legend. The best is probably *Live In Amsterdam*, recorded in 1970 on their last tour together. The only unreleased song is a version of *Silver Haired Daddy* and I don't think that Simon and Garfunkel tackling a 40 year old Gene Autry song – albeit beautifully – gives any real insight into their craft. The thing one notices in listening to S&G bootlegs, is the repetition of key songs. They were so professional, though, that there is frankly little difference between a 1966 live recording of, say *The Sounds Of Silence* and a 1970 version. It is, of course, rewarding to compare Paul Simon's solo version of the song from the 1965 *Songbook*, and his later interpretation with the Jesse Dixon Singers from 1974. But, like so many artists, their real energies went into recording, and the best place to hear Simon and Garfunkel's songs performed the way they wanted them to sound are on their CBS albums.

June 1972 was the time that saw Simon and Garfunkel back together again in concert. Along with a number of other notable partnerships from the Sixties – like Mike Nichols and Elaine May, Peter, Paul and Mary – S&G appeared at a fund raising concert for Senator George McGovern. Warren Beatty had helped organise a number of shows for the Democratic candidate's campaign which saw a number of rock luminaries lend a hand.

The Madison Square Gardens benefit was not a success. Simon and Garfunkel ran through a perfunctory selection of their best known songs, and Rolling Stone acidly noted: "They stood at their mikes looking straight ahead, like two commuters clutching adjacent straps on the morning train!" Beatty's campaign was equally as unsuccessful: in November, Richard Nixon was elected by the biggest popular vote in American political history.

Simon eventually chose to tour with a hand-chosen group of musicians to promote his album. Garfunkel, with **Carnal Knowledge** on release, could now turn his attentions to his debut. Clive Davis at CBS recalls Garfunkel "equivocating" about the sort of music he was to feature. Obviously, he was not a writer, so the songs would have to come from outside. Garfunkel originally wanted to record an album combining classical and contemporary music, then an album's worth of church music, then Greek music. Davis eventually persuaded him to do an album featuring songs by contemporary writers, which he duly did, at a cost of two hundred thousand dollars. Davis was understandably concerned about the cost of *Angel Clare*, but the ever precise Garfunkel was confident: "I haven't lost my perspective. The album is taking a long time, but I'm fully in control." Even when told it would have to sell at least a quarter of a million copies to break even, Garfunkel was sanguine: "Don't worry about a thing", he assured Davis, "it's in the bag." *Angel Clare* went on to sell a million copies within a year.

Angel Clare (the title comes from a character in Thomas Hardy's **Tess Of The d'Urbervilles**, a character epitomising innocence) reunited Garfunkel with Roy Halee, as well as other familiar names from the S&G days, like Larry Knechtel, Joe Osborn, Hal Blaine and Paul Simon.

The album sees Garfunkel pursuing his idea of a rock-classical marriage, notably on *Feuilles-Oh/Do Space Men Pass Dead Souls On Their Way To The Moon?* which was written by J.S. Bach and Garfunkel's then wife, Linda Grossman. Church music was also in evidence with Garfunkel's use of the Grace Cathedral Choir. On its release, *Angel Clare* was criticised for its lushness. While many commented on Simon's funky debut, *Angel Clare* relied on swathing the singer's pure voice with lavish arrangements. It is a comfortable, assured debut, which appealed to the millions who loved the sweetness of *Bridge Over Troubled Water*. There's no denying the innate quality of Garfunkel's voice, but for all its ambitions, *Angel Clare* is little more than a high quality, easy listening album. Randy Newman's caustic *Old Man* is transformed here into a syrupy ballad and the beautiful, traditional *Barbara Allen* loses any emotional impact through its lush arrangement and Garfunkel's insistence at multi-tracking his unique voice.

Garfunkel also illustrated the diversity of his musical tastes by including the "criss-cross rhythms" of Osibisa on *Woyaya*; Bach on *Feuilles-Oh* and contemporary songs from Van Morrison, Jim Webb and Randy Newman. The album's best track, *Mary Was An Only Child*, is a driving pop song, with interesting lyrics from Albert Hammond, Mike Hazlewood and Jorge (Los Incas) Milchberg.

The commercial success of *Angel Clare* must have been due as much to the public's curiosity as to the album's topical mellowness. What was apparent was that Simon and Garfunkel were further apart on record than their initial separation suggested.

Simon ushered in 1973 with a book, **The Songs Of Paul Simon** which was a record of his best known work and also featured an introductory essay from the composer. It acted as a resumé of Simon's career to date, which continued apace with the release of his second solo album in May, 1973. Considering the usual two year lapse between albums, a new Paul Simon album so soon after his debut was quite an achievement. Simon was aware of that too, as he told Melody Maker's Loraine Alterman: "An album in less than 18 months for me is lightning."

There Goes Rhymin' Simon, from its very title, was evidence of Paul Simon shaking off his serious poet image. The cover was a collage, illustrating the song titles, done in a deliberately sloppy way, which Simon and Garfunkel would never have passed. It marked a complete catalogue of Simon's career, from the Tom and Jerry days (the teenage Simon in the top right hand corner) to the picture illustrating *St Judy's Comet*, with Simon cradling his young son, Harper. The proof of the wheel coming full circle was evident in the songs themselves: the Jerry Landis days were evoked on *Was A Sunny Day*, where the chorus of "She called him Speedoo/But his Christian name was Mr Earl" comes directly from the Cadillacs 1955 hit *Speedoo* (which Ry Cooder later covered on his 1980 *Borderline* album). The preceding song on *Rhymin' Simon* though, *American Tune*, was as intellectually demanding and perfectly constructed as anything Simon and Garfunkel had ever attempted.

American Tune was the album's most ambitious song, like Garfunkel, Simon also borrowed from Bach, the song's tune comes from the *Sacred Heart* section of *The Saint Matthew Passion*. It is a moving, timely song, a reflection on the state of the nation during the uncertainty which the Watergate revelations induced.

It is a consoling appraisal of achievements during "the age's most uncertain hours". It's Simon musing on the individual in a society betrayed by its President. Ostensibly dark, with battered souls and shattered dreams, *American Tune* is an affirmation, a statement of hope, particularly the final verse, a testimony that America will survive. The shifting Statue of Liberty is a long way from the cars on the New Jersey Turnpike. *American Tune* was an astonishing, mature statement, even from a writer as talented as Paul Simon. Rolling Stone obviously felt so too, when they voted *American Tune* Song of the Year for 1973.

The remainder of the songs were deliberately lighter in content. *Kodachrome* was a pacey song, with an ambiguous chorus "A Nikon camera" or is it "an icon"? It rattles along, preferring the illusion of a colour photograph to the reality of the black and white world. *Take Me To The Mardi Gras* is beautifully atmospheric with the Reverend Juter's piercing falsetto well to the fore, conjuring up New Orleans in all its flamboyant colour. *Was A Sunny Day* is another evocative song, conveying a joy of being young, taking a childish delight in the weather and "the birdies in the trees" and the soul-saving rock 'n' roll pouring like honey from the radio. That same childish simplicity is more obvious on Simon's lullaby, *St Judy's Comet*, a lovely, lilting song to lull his son to sleep. It manages to avoid twee sentimentality and includes the nicely self-deprecating lines: "'Cause if I can't sing my boy to sleep/Well, 't makes your famous daddy look so dumb."

Less successful are songs like *One Man's Ceiling Is Another Man's Floor* and *Learn How To Fall*, one idea songs, similar to *Run That Body Down*. *Something So Right* is a nice ballad, but suffers from the clumsy parallel Simon draws with the Great Wall of China and his own emotional wall. *Tenderness* lacks bite, although benefitting from an acute observation that "there's no tenderness beneath your honesty."

Musically, *Rhymin' Simon* again displays Simon's ability to assimilate. He had been particularly impressed by the Staples Singers' record *I'll Take You There*, and decided to try out the same musicians at the Muscle Shoals studios. He was so impressed with the facilities that instead of only recording *Take Me To The Mardi Gras* there, he ended up recording over half the album at the famous Alabama studios. Simon's love of gospel music is apparent and his use of the Dixie Hummingbirds was so suitable for his new material, notably on the rousing *Loves Me Like A Rock*. The growing interest in jazz is there too, from Quincy Jones arrangement for *Something So Right* to the use of the Onward Brass Band on *Mardi Gras*.

The Staple Singers at The
Appollo Theatre at
New York

The Roches – Maggie, Terre
and Suzie

To promote the album, Simon took a hand-picked package of excellent musicians on a world tour including Urubamba and the Jesse Dixon Singers. With the presence of the Dixon singers, familiar material took on a funkier, gospel feel, which worked audaciously well on songs like *The Sounds Of Silence*. Simon was as precise in recreating his songs live as he was in the studio and he even managed to overcome the Royal Albert Hall's notoriously bad acoustics. Nineteen seventy three also saw one of Art Garfunkel's rare solo appearances as a performer without Paul Simon, when in October he appeared at a CBS convention. He brought the house down with his rendering of *Bridge Over Troubled Water* which had virtually become the company's anthem during their problems with payola that had led to Clive Davis's departure.

Simon, meanwhile, produced a single for the Roche Sisters called *If You Could Not Empty Your Pockets, You Could Not Make The Change*, which was never released in Britain and was not a hit in the States. *Groundhog* was a rare, unrecorded Simon song, which he donated to Peter Yarrow (of Peter, Paul and Mary) for his solo album *That's Enough For Me* in 1973.

Simon also produced an album for Urubamba (which featured two members of Los Incas) and the album was praised for its lack of obtrusive production. His 1973 concert tour was recorded for a live album, which was eventually released as *Live Rhymin'* in 1974. As someone ambivalent about his life's work, Simon explained his reasons for touring to Melody Maker in May 1973: "I just decided to do something so I'd just be getting off my ass . . . I'll go out and I'll sing my songs and I'll try and sing in tune, and basically that's what I have to offer. People either want to hear me sing my songs or they don't so I feel that nobody will be expecting any more out of me than that." Such a statement was hardly that of a committed performer. Compare Simon with Bruce Springsteen who puts a similar, dedicated effort into recording his albums, but also positively thrives on performing live.

By 1973, Simon had been performing for the best part of sixteen years, starting off with Tom and Jerry, through his busking round the British folk clubs, his concerts with Garfunkel and in his own right as a solo performer. As creator of some of the most haunting, personal songs of his generation, performing them live was a necessary evil. That is not to say he has ever shirked from putting on the best show he is capable of giving. As a creative artist, Simon felt the constant desire to move forward, to improve, but that ambition can be constantly thwarted when performing before an audience hungry for the older, more familiar songs. For an artist, it is a difficult process to compile a set which satisfies him, featuring new material with which he is justifiably proud, and still catering to the audience's demand for older songs which mean so much to them. Simon is obviously proud of all his songs but has phases of fondness. In a 1968 interview he said: "They're pictures of me . . . I can say this song is a *better* song, but I like them all, because they all came out of a time in my life. Then times change, so I write different songs. But it would be like saying 'Which do you prefer, being 20 or 23?'"

Judith Piepe summed up Simon's dilemma when I spoke to her in 1982: "A performer, a singer, *has* to be extrovert . . . But a writer is introvert, because you can't create in a crowd. And a singer-songwriter is always on a horrible see-saw." With Paul Simon, that "see-saw" was perhaps more apparent than with many of his contemporaries. His songs evoked a strong, personal response in his audience while millions were sympathetic to the sentiments he so coherently expressed. Simon admitted all his songs were a part of his life but he had moved on. His audience, though, felt that Simon's songs were companions through their lives and, like any old friend, it's always nice to see them again. Simon managed to balance his live sets with generous slices of Simon and Garfunkel history, as well as more recent songs. Yet it would be ridiculous for someone now in their forties to sing an adolescent song like *I Am A Rock* or even the collegiate *Dangling Conversation*.

Simon told Chris Charlesworth in 1975 that he felt a live album was almost obligatory in evaluating any artist's work "to keep a sense of continuity." Nineteen seventy four was certainly a year when continuity was needed. Neither Simon nor Garfunkel had any fresh material for release, so *Live Rhymin'* in March was welcomed. It also marked the first official opportunity to hear Paul Simon perform his songs, live on record.

The album is as precisely recorded as one would expect from Paul Simon, with Simon allowing his backing musicians the opportunity to extend to their full range. Predictably, it's the old S&G songs which gain the loudest cheers, all Simon has to do is pick the opening notes of *Homeward Bound*, and any audience, from Widnes to Woy Woy will erupt. On *Live Rhymin'* he hesitantly sings the first line of *The Boxer*, waits for the inevitable applause then continues. As a performer it must be exhilerating, as well as slightly infuriating. Simon's still dogged by the 'spokesman for a generation' tag for, at the end of side two, someone shouts "say a few words." "Well," says Simon, temporarily phased, "I hope we can all live together . . ." It's enough, the spokesman has spoken, and the audience acknowledge his sage words with applause. *Live Rhymin'* offers an opportunity to delight in Simon's ability as a guitarist. His talent in that area is frequently overlooked, of course he's best known as a writer of superb songs, but anyone who can breeze through Davy Graham's complex *Anji* or the Bachian complexities of *American Tune* on a simple acoustic guitar is obviously adept. Simon could only write songs with a guitar and he had recurring problems with an infection of one of his hands which had curtailed his writing. This happened in late 1973. Consequently he had no material written for a new album, which was one reason behind the release of the live album.

A point of interest on *Live Rhymin'* was the additional extra verse on *The Boxer*, which S&G had been including in performances for years but never featured on record. It's a verse that was frequently extracted to comment on the 1981 reunion, particularly the line "After changes upon changes, we are more or less the same." It's really little more than an adaptation of Alphonse Karr's famous maxim: "The more things change, the more they are the same." The remainder of the added verse hardly reach new heights in the Simon philosophy: "I am older than I once was, and younger than I'll be/ But that's not unusual . . ."

Live albums are frequently used by artists as periods of transition; an artist caught shedding his past, promoting his present and indicating his future. It's certainly true with *Live Rhymin'*. Gospel pre-

PETER SIMON

dominates the album which, in the case of *Bridge Over Troubled Water*, is repaying the debt, as the song originally sprang from gospel roots, and it's awesome to hear the Jesse Dixon Singers turning the song into a celebration as they chant "I will ease your mind" at the song's climax.

Transitional as the album was, the bias was still over Simon's shoulder, six of the twelve songs were from the S&G catalogue, although one can sense Simon's pride in the vigorous rendition of *Loves Me Like A Rock*, and the swinging versions of his own recent songs like *Mother And Child Reunion*.

For me, that period of Simon's career was characterised in a story Lon Goddard – then looking after Simon's press for CBS – told me. He heard Simon was recording *American Tune* at Morgan Studios in London, and went down as an official representative of Simon's British record company "to see if there was anything he wanted." Simon was friendly enough in his dealings with Lon, but when asked if he needed any help, curtly responded: "I can look after myself."

The following year, 1975, saw Simon and Garfunkel growing further apart musically. It was also, ironically, the year that brought them back together on record.

Chapter Seven

Chronologically, Simon and Garfunkel couldn't have timed it better. It had been five years since they had last appeared properly on record together, it was exactly halfway through the decade, the Sixties had become a memory, and Simon and Garfunkel were part of that collective memory. *My Little Town* coincided perfectly; it also happened to be one of Simon's strongest ever songs. CBS weren't slow off the mark to realise the commercial possibilities. The fact that both Simon *and* Garfunkel had solo albums scheduled for 1975 was too good an opportunity to miss. Both had sold respectably enough during their solo careers, but the public craved the magic combination.

Simon had *My Little Town* stockpiled, and offered it to Garfunkel with the caustic observation: "I volunteered a nasty song, because he hadn't been singing any nasty songs lately." Garfunkel was delighted with the song, and invited Simon to help him sing it, which resulted in the eagerly anticipated Simon and Garfunkel reunion. Consequentially, *My Little Town* appears on Garfunkel's *Breakaway* album, and Simon's *Still Crazy After All These Years*. Such calculation ensures, as they say, maximum sales potential.

Garfunkel was still embracing the work of contemporary writers, and was obviously pleased that one of their peers – and his former partner – would donate a song to him. He remembered the circumstances to Chris Charlesworth: "He had this song that he was working on and it looked like he wasn't going to use it on his album and he knew that I liked the song . . . I started working on the song, knowing all the while that Paul Simon, not being too prolific a writer, was probably going to need the song himself. Sure enough, he figured later that it would be nice on his album too, so we started working on a harmony version because I thought that the middle part was ideally suited to the old S&G blend, and I felt like harmonising with Paul because I hadn't done that in years."

My Little Town works superbly well. Simon denied that it was autobiographical, but it perfectly captures the frustration of small town life and the tense potential of growing up in such a stifling environment struck a responsive chord in many listeners. It was a joy to hear the old, familiar Simon and Garfunkel harmonies weaving together again, particularly round such a strong song.

The first verse sharply depicts the misplaced allegiance and claustrophobia of the little town in question: *flying* the bike past the factory gates, the laundry in the dirty breeze, the black rainbow of desperation. All contribute to the song's taut atmosphere. Simon saves the killer punch for the last round "I never meant nothin', I was just my father's son . . . twitching like a finger on the trigger of a gun." It's all there, in that brilliant, coiled image – the hereditary frustration and repression; the belief in yourself and *your* abilities, which can never be realised, not in that unimaginative little town.

While the evidence of a Simon and Garfunkel reunion fascinated the press, it was obviously only temporary. The tenseness which had contributed to the break up was still there, and the musical differences were apparent. Just play *Breakaway* and *Still Crazy* side by side to see that. *My Little Town* had only been intended as a one-off, which was how Simon and Garfunkel's relationship remained for the next five years.

Simon appeared, uncharacteristically, at Phil Ochs' *War Is Over* celebration in Central Park in May 1975. Ochs had arranged the event to commemorate America's withdrawal from Vietnam, and Simon performed briefly alongside Pete Seeger and Joan Baez. Simon also wrote the score for Warren Beatty's film **Shampoo**. As previously mentioned, Simon had been inundated with offers for film soundtracks following **The Graduate** but stoically refused them all. The attractions of **Shampoo** were obvious: he had worked with Beatty on the McGovern fund-raising events and the political aspects of the film must have appealed to Simon's liberal conscience. It's only a shame his music wasn't used more fully, and that **Shampoo** wasn't a better film. It concentrates on the sexual mores of a languid L.A. hairdresser, an essential part of the life of the Laurel Canyon parasites, personified by Beatty's smooth, androgynous character. Way below the surface was an examination of American politics. In the light of the Watergate revelations, **Shampoo** could have been a timely exposition of political deceitfulness. Instead, it concentrated on Nixon's 1968 election victory and gave Beatty and co-writer Robert Towne plenty of opportunity to indulge in their liberal fantasies. A lot of contemporary music (the Beatles, Buffalo Springfield) was incorporated, but Simon's actual contribution was limited to (unpaid) snatches of humming. *Have A Good Time* and *Silent Eyes* – which were used on the *Still Crazy* album – were intended for the film, but were never fully used.

Simon's creative career had reached a crossroads, he told Chris Charlesworth in November 1975: "I don't think I'm going to start work on another album. I think I'm going to do something else . . . A show, a movie. Rather than write ten songs and sing them, I'll try and write my songs *for* something."

With such statements, Simon was laying the groundwork for his film of **One Trick Pony**, but the three month lay-off he intended stretched into a five year sabbatical. Simon obviously saw his creative life becoming a ritual: an album every eighteen months and a tour to promote the album. He felt the need to flex his creative muscles, to attempt something on a larger scale. With his typical attention to detail, and few obligations outstanding, Simon applied his energies to film.

The fact that both Simon and Garfunkel's latest solo albums were issued simultaneously, *and* the fact that they were back together again on *My Little Town*, led to much speculation about their future together. Both were swift to deny any permanence but they did

With Gilda Radner of
Saturday Night Live fame

appear together again towards the end of 1975. They sang together on the late night American satire show **Saturday Night Live** in September, and Garfunkel was a 'special guest' at Simon's show at New York's Avery Fisher Hall in October, joining him for five songs.

The main points of interest, though, were their new albums. Garfunkel's *Breakaway* is his best solo effort to date, and one which generated a massive world-wide hit single. *I Only Have Eyes For You* was an old Hollywood standard, which the Flamingoes had scored with in 1959. Garfunkel surrounded himself with some impressive names for his second solo album – David Crosby and Graham Nash, the Beach Boys' Bruce Johnston, Booker T's Steve Cropper and Little Feat's Bill Payne. The songs were mainly chosen by producer Richard Perry and were ideally suited to Garfunkel's distinctive voice. Lushly produced, *Breakaway* is an ideal companion to those who so admired his voice when interpreting Simon's softer songs.

Lush and restful, it's high quality muzak for the Woodstock generation, a soft rock masterpiece, which swiftly found favour with a new generation that admired Elton John and Fleetwood Mac. From Stevie Wonder's *I Believe (When I Fall In Love It Will Be Forever)* to Stephen Bishop's *Looking For The Right One*, it seemed as though Art Garfunkel had finally found a form of music he could make his own. Producer Richard Perry was quoted as saying it was his own personal favourite of all the albums he had produced.

There's no denying the soaring purity of Garfunkel's singing, and on *Breakaway* he sounded more confident in his own abilities. Spencer Leigh pointed out the contrasts between Paul Simon's bitter memories of childhood on *My Little Town* and Bruce Johnston's unashamedly nostalgic view on *Disney Girls*. For Simon, there's "nothing but the dead and dying" back there, Johnston opines "Reality, it's not for me . . . But fantasy world, and Disney girls, I'm coming back." Garfunkel renders a lovely version of the latter, a song that first appeared on the Beach Boys classic *Surf's Up* album in 1971.

Obviously all of Paul Simon's new songs were going on his solo album, and Garfunkel began using a coterie of regular writers. *Breakaway* saw his initial use of a Gallagher and Lyle song. The talented Scottish duo had been house-writers for the Beatles' Apple Organisation, and wrote the excellent *When I'm Dead And Gone* for McGuinness-Flint in 1970. Garfunkel achieved a hit with their *Heart In New York* six years later. Stephen Bishop was another writer Garfunkel was fond of, and *Breakaway* also saw him cover the former Frank Sinatra collaborator, Antonio Carlos Jobim's song, *Waters Of March*. Garfunkel was fond of the song, which he felt was a child's view of the world, which goes some way in negating the pretentiousness of the lyrics.

The success of *I Only Have Eyes For You* obviously stimulated interest in the album. Even without a regular supply of Paul Simon songs, *Breakaway* indicated that Art Garfunkel could carve a separate solo cateer for himself.

Simon was divorced ("without bitterness") from his wife Peggy in 1975. It was a decisive event, and one which many people felt shaped the songs on his fourth solo album, *Still Crazy After All These Years*. Of his new songs, Simon told Chris Charlesworth: "They're personal, but not autobiographical . . . I'm vaguely talking about my life, but I'm not *specifically* talking about my life . . . They reflect

BOB LEAFE

what's happening, but not the entirety of the thing."

The *Still Crazy* album was Simon's most mature musical statement to date and displayed, yet again, his keenness to work with different types of musicians. But still people kept dogging him about an S&G reunion which Simon quashed when he told Melody Maker about *My Little Town*: "It was very tense at first, but after that, really pleasant . . . I don't think you could bring back Simon and Garfunkel and go back to where it was . . . I would like to sing a song with Artie, but not as a permanent partnership. I would like to sing a song with Phoebe Snow. I would like to be able to sing a song with the Dixie Hummingbirds. That's the way I like to record now." That eclecticism was evident on Simon's new album. *Still Crazy* was a confident, assured work, with Simon able to reflect on childhood, relationships, religion, death and baseball with assurance. He told Crawdaddy's Timothy White in early 1976: "People thirty years old wonder why they're not getting off on popular music the way they once did and it's because nobody's singing for them. When you reach a certain age you're not naive any more. Everything I write can't be a philosophical truth, but it certainly isn't innocent – because I'm not.

"Music is forever; music should grow and mature with you, following you right on up until you die." Paul Simon was in his mid-thirties when *Still Crazy* was made, recently divorced and a proud father. The songs on the album obviously sprang from personal experience, but Simon had the ability to distance himself from the characters in his songs. Dylan's *Blood On The Tracks* album was released the same year, a harrowing, intensely personal collection of songs about Dylan's own separation from his wife. Simon's album is nowhere near as uncomfortable to listen to as Dylan's catharsis but therein lies its strength. The discipline and structure of Simon's songs, where every word counts, adds to their durability. The album's title track is a perfect example, a wry and wistful account of a lovers' reunion, with a jerky, paranoid reflection in the final verse. Of sitting by the window, and fearing he'll "do some damage, one fine day", which recalls the final verse of *My Little Town*. But here, Simon is convinced "I would not be convicted by a jury of my peers", a flawless final rhyme with "still crazy after all these years." A touching and quietly disturbing song.

I Do It For Your Love is a deceptively simple song. Its detailed disintegration of a marriage (like *Overs* seven years before) is all the more remarkable for its succinctness. "All that winter we shared a cold/Drank all the orange juice that we could hold" is a glowing, warm image of young love, which has gone by the final verse. "The sting of reason/The splash of tears/The northern and southern hemispheres/Love emerges and it disappears" is an opaque, quietly moving rhyme which Simon sings with touching resignation.

50 Ways To Leave Your Lover is one of the few songs where the verses are stronger than the chorus, the rhyming of "intrude", "misconstrued" and "crude" is masterly, whereas the rhymes with mens' names palls after the initial novelty. The song came about though, as simple rhymes Simon made up to amuse his young son, so perhaps it's unfair to be overtly critical.

Night Game is an inscrutable song, steeped in one of Simon's few unrealised ambitions, to be a successful baseball player. Asked by Rolling Stone what he would like to have been if he hadn't made it as

a successful songwriter, Simon earnestly replied: "A relief pitcher!" Mickey Mantle and Joe DiMaggio were as much heroes of Simon's as any writer or performer. *Night Game* is a quirky account of a pitcher's death, and the ritual attached to his funeral, complete with odd, poetic intrusions, like the chilling image of the stars "as white as bone."

Gone At Last is a searing slab of gospel and Simon's best venture into that field. Originally intended as a duet with Bette Midler, Simon eventually recorded it with Phoebe Snow whose first album he greatly admired. It has been a frequent highlight of Simon's live shows with the tiny Simon consoled by a trio of large negro mamas. *Some Folks' Lives Roll Easy* touches on religion, which is a theme running through the album, and here Simon ruefully acknowledges that "Most folks never catch their stars."

Have A Good Time manages to suggest Simon was doing just that, a jazzy excursion into growing old, but with none of the bleakness of *Old Friends*. Simon's resigned that one more year has been hung on the line, and recognises that "My life's a mess/I should be depressed" – but what the hell, have a good time! "Paranoia strikes deep in the heartland/But I think it's all overdone." sounds like a deliberately iconoclastic Simon line, the prophet of paranoia renouncing his past, and ending with the materialistic exhortation that we "God bless the good we was given/And God bless the US of A/And God bless our standard of livin'/Let's keep it that way." A long way from the isolated poet, with only his books and his poetry to protect him.

You're Kind is a bittersweet song, about rescue, disillusion and parting, redeemed by Simon's laconic humour. The failure of the relationship is attributed to the fact that "I like to sleep with the window open/And you keep the window closed/So goodbye . . ." The sort of sentiment you'd expect from one of Woody Allen's brittle New York comedies.

The last we would hear from Paul Simon for five long years was the enigmatic *Silent Eyes*, a devout testament to Simon's Jewish faith. Judith Piepe felt that Simon's Jewishness played a sizable part in much of his creative work. There have certainly been many Biblical references in his songs, going back to *Bleecker Street*, eleven years before. Religious references before were usually restricted to specific instances, songs like *Blessed* and *Seven O'Clock News/Silent Night* but *Silent Eyes* finds Jerusalem calling Simon by name, calling him as a witness "To stand before the eyes of God/And speak what was done." An avowal of faith, of purgatory leading to the final confrontation – a subdued and dignified climax.

With *Still Crazy* Simon had, yet again, expanded his musical horizons. Chuck Israels and David Sorin Collyer, whom he thanked on the sleeve for having helped him with his music, were two jazzmen under whom he had studied composition and arrangement in New York. Simon was credited as arranging several of the tracks on the album. Simon himself never intended his absence to stretch out so long but significantly, it coincided with the rise of the new wave.

The care and attention Simon and Garfunkel lavished on their albums was the very antithesis of punk's aggression. *Breakaway* and *Still Crazy After All These Years* sounded like the last, lavish messages from the mansions of the rock aristocracy. Outside the walls, the punks were seething.

Chapter Eight

The same month that Paul Simon played the London Palladium in November 1975, the Sex Pistols played their debut gig at St Martin's College down the road. Simon told the New Musical Express that December that he was most "comfortable" playing to venues of 7 or 8,000 people. In that statement lay the seeds of the punk rebellion.

After the sanitised, commercialised teenybop groups of the early Seventies, the post-Beatles generation had no real heroes of their own. As someone, probably Malcolm McLaren, put it "They were tired of listening to their elder brother's Pink Floyd albums and smoking his old joints." Rock 'n' roll had moved from the intimacy of clubs to impersonal stadia, the success of the mega-bands meant they had to play bigger and bigger venues. To be seen to be putting on a show meant a growing theatricality and spectacle, which sacrificed the original aggressive power of rock music. The Pistols were the tip of the punk iceberg, within weeks, hundreds of bands had sprung up all over the UK. They wanted to rekindle rock's original fiery power. Punk's great strength was that anybody could do it, studios were suddenly accessible, independent distributors and fanzines meant that even the monolithic record companies and music papers could be bypassed. Punk stripped away the mystique of the music business, there was no need to adhere to the old heroes, the punks created their own, literally overnight.

Musically, the punk revolution made many of the old guard rock idols look to their laurels. The punks wanted energy and commitment, they didn't want 18 months spent recording an album. It was a traumatic time for music, there was little space for lyrical subtlety (save for Elvis Costello or Ian Dury). What was wanted was energy, *now*!

It was an attitude the precise and cultured Art Garfunkel simply could not understand. Waxing lyrical about Fleetwood Mac's *Tusk* to Chris Hodenfield in a Rolling Stone interview of 1980, he said: "That kind of record making is right up my alley. Where are the recording artists who stay in the studio for the labour of love, way beyond what's practical or sensible in terms of profit? Where are the artists who completely slip out of corporate mentality, who just stretch out in the studio and make it sound the way they know it should sound?" They were not on the streets doing it. You may argue the toss about its musical pedigree, but punk saved rock 'n' roll from disappearing up its own pretensions. While setting out to destroy the bloated concept of Seventies rock 'n' roll, the Sex Pistols ironically

With Stevie Nicks of Fleetwood Mac

BOB LEAFE

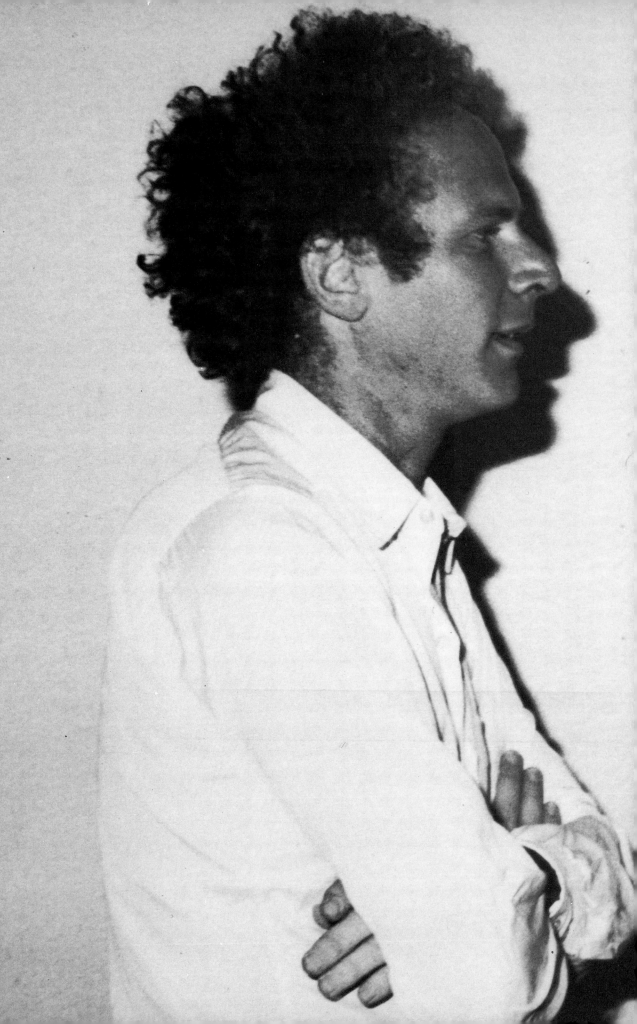

proved its greatest asset. Their attitude, though, didn't automatically preclude the artists Garfunkel favoured still lavishing care and attention on their product, Fleetwood Mac, the Eagles and Queen still approached each album like a Cecil B. de Mille production.

Garfunkel proved himself disastrously out of touch when he confessed to Stephen Holden, again in Rolling Stone, in 1981: "I haven't followed what's been happening in pop music for the last five years, because for me it's *not* happening." An arrogant and unbelievably blinkered statement from someone in a five year period that had seen the development of Springsteen, Costello, the Pistols, the Clash, the Jam and many more. Simon proved himself hipper, checking out gigs by Springsteen, the B52s and the Clash – "But I had to leave the concert to protect my ears", unknowingly confirming Joe Strummer's harsh maxim that "If it's too loud, you're too old!"

Once his film and recording commitments were honoured, Art Garfunkel had spent considerable time travelling around Europe – Scotland, Ireland and Greece. Essentially a private person, he seemed to thrive on the anonymity these European trips gave him; the hysteria that surrounded Simon and Garfunkel was anathema to him. The fact that he had chosen to study mathematics and architecture suggested a man who delighted in the order of things. That appreciation of discipline and order was reflected in the scrupulous attention to detail Garfunkel applied to his albums.

It was Garfunkel who broke the three year S&G silence, in 1978, with the release of *Watermark*, an album which was little more than a showcase for the songs of Jim Webb. Webb was well known when still a teenager. He had supplied hit songs for Glen Campbell, the Fifth Dimension and Richard Harris. Scrupulously noted on the sleeve is the fact that *Watermark* took over a year to make.

The only two non-Webb songs on the album are Sam Cooke's 1958 hit *What A Wonderful World* and the almost traditional *She Moves Through The Fair*. Despite repeated hearings, *Watermark* is the aural equivalent of drowning in syrup. Garfunkel has one of the purest, clearest voices in rock, and despite his obvious misunderstanding of the medium, he could use that marvellous voice to great effect on the right sort of song. *She Moves Through The Fair* is a classic example and Garfunkel was obviously, rightly, impressed with the Chieftains classical complexity in dealing with traditional Irish music. He went to Dublin to record his version of the *Padriac Colum* with them. But instead of letting them shine in their own right, Garfunkel, as producer, swamps their originality with an unnecessarily lush arrangement which completely buries the original beauty. (Just listen to Fairport Convention's 1968 version of the song to hear how it can be sympathetically treated.)

The same applies to *Wonderful World*. As a song, Cooke's original matches Chuck Berry's wry depiction of Fifties' teenage plight, a litany of incomprehension concerning school subjects, ending with the lovely line "Don't know nothin' 'bout nothin' at all/Girl, it's you that I've been thinkin' of." Yet the song's impish spark is deluged under the multi-tracked voices of Simon, Garfunkel and James Taylor. What could have been a prime example of Art Garfunkel showing his roots becomes a langorous version which manages to destroy the charm of the original. And yes, it was another Simon and Garfunkel reunion, but quite what Simon was doing as party to this

Watership Down – *Bright Eyes* was its theme song

travesty is beyond me, he went into print saying he felt Sam Cooke's voice "beats them all", and yet here he was doing one of his songs scant justice.

Of the remaining Webb songs, they are ideally suited for Art Garfunkel. Webb proved his ability to write classic pop songs early in his career – *Wichita Lineman, McArthur Park* – but here he seems to have fallen into that awful morass of AOR rock. The epitaph for *Watermark* is contained on Webb's *Mr Shuck 'n' Jive*: "If you can get yourself together, kindly write a criticism of this song/How it's exquisitely constructed, yet mechanical, and somehow slightly wrong!"

Garfunkel had patently lost touch with his rock 'n' roll roots, and didn't seem confident enough to trust his own ability in choosing material. Of course, if you're used to the consistent quality of songs by Paul Simon, it must be difficult to adapt. Yet Garfunkel seems locked into those soft rock options offered by Webb, Stephen Bishop and Gallagher and Lyle. He never stretches himself on record, swathing the purity of his voice in double tracking and unnecessarily lavish arrangements.

Garfunkel's self-confessed ignorance of recent rock developments has meant an unwillingness to experiment with new writers. Sympathetic writers like Rodney Crowell, Jackson Browne, Joan Armatrading and Tom Waits have a number of songs which would be ideally suited to Garfunkel's voice. It would be rewarding to hear him stretch himself on new material, to tackle an album of traditional material, or the *best* contemporary writers, instead of taking the easy option.

As a solo singer, Garfunkel hit the big time again when his version of *Bright Eyes* reached number one in 1979. It was the theme song (written by Womble creator Mike Batt) from an animated film about rabbits. Garfunkel had certainly come a long way from Bleecker Street. His fourth solo album, *Fate For Breakfast* (1979) simply confirmed Garfunkel as the Soft Rock King. There's a nice cover of Cliff Richard's 1975 hit, *Miss You Nights*, which is mercifully sparse by Garfunkel's standards, otherwise, it was the same as it ever was, production line muzak, which failed to recognise Garfunkel's greatest asset – his voice. But even there he took fewer and fewer risks, there's a nice scat break on *Mr Shuck 'n' Jive*, but otherwise he takes the easy option of smothering any sincerity or passion with strings. It was a pity Paul Simon couldn't have found time to have written more 'nasty' songs for his erstwhile partner.

Judith Piepe knew Garfunkel well from his days in England and remembered him thus: "Artie was in many ways Paul's other voice, his sounding board. I told Artie in '65 that he must do some things without Paul, or he would never be himself. Artie was aware of his dependence on Paul who, at that time, was not aware of his dependance on Artie."

Garfunkel's solo formula continued with *Scissors Cut* in 1981. With a galaxy of star names (including an undistinguished vocal from Simon on Jim Webb's *In Cars*, which inexplicably tailed off with a snatch of Dylan's *Girl From The North Country*), the album groans under treacly songs from Jim Webb, Gallagher and Lyle and Clifford T. Ward. From the soul-less arrangements to the Flaubert quote on the inner sleeve, the album brings into question just how much Garfunkel actually contributed to the Simon and Garfunkel partnership. At least when recording with Simon – like Lennon and McCartney – the two seemed to balance each other's excesses. Adrift from that balance, Garfunkel seemed aimless. His announcement in 1981 that he had no further solo albums actually came as quite a relief to those who still treasured Simon and Garfunkel's legacy.

Even Garfunkel's acting career was in abeyance for eight years. Garfunkel made no film between **Carnal Knowledge** in 1971 and the 1979 **Bad Timing**. Director Nicolas Roeg had quite a reputation working with rock stars, he had put Mick Jagger through his paces in **Performance** in 1970, and confused everyone, including David Bowie with **The Man Who Fell To Earth** in 1976. Garfunkel forged a strong friendship with Roeg, with the result that **Bad Timing** is his best film to date. It's a taut, psychological drama, which proved an arduous experience for Garfunkel, as he found himself becoming immersed in his character. He spent much of 1979 filming in Vienna, and later admitted that it had been "the hardest year of my life". Garfunkel's wife Linda sued him for divorce, and his long-time girlfriend Laurie Bird committed suicide in their apartment while he was on location filming.

In a stark, confessional interview with Chris Hodenfield of Rolling Stone in October 1980, Garfunkel spoke of his love for Laurie Bird (to whom *Scissors Cut* is dedicated) and how he drew faith from the

Paul Simon (top centre) with the five other co-stars from **Annie Hall** (from upper right clockwise) Colleen Dewhurst, Carol Kane, Tony Roberts, Shelley Duval and Janet Margolin

Art as Alex in **Bad Timing**

KOBAL

Bible to sustain him through that tragic period in his life.

Garfunkel was rightly proud of his performance in **Bad Timing** but the film was not the success it deserved to be and it was virtually ignored in America, although European audiences were more encouraging. He engaged an agent to find further suitable film roles but has not appeared on screen since. Garfunkel also watched the *Scissors Cut* album and *Heart In New York* single disappear without trace. With his singing and acting careers in limbo, Garfunkel began hanging out again with Paul Simon.

The release of *Still Crazy After All These Years* in October 1975 saw the expiry of Simon's contract with CBS. Although none of his subsequent solo albums had matched the enormous sales of *Bridge*, Simon was a steady seller with an excellent reputation, and CBS would be sorry to lose him from their roster. As he had explained before, he wanted to take time off from simply writing and recording songs for another album. The embryonic idea for the film of **One Trick Pony** was in his mind, and Simon felt that Warner Bros, with their sizable film division, would probably be a more sympathetic company. Simon was surprised at CBS's reaction to his leaving the fold: "Their reaction was unpredictably severe", he told the Sunday Times, "and I felt they were hostile to me on a personal level. I've never in my entire career had an enemy, and it was all very upsetting to me." Simon may have been slightly mollified with the knowledge that his contract with Warners guaranteed him somewhere in the region of fourteen million dollars for his first seven albums. Simon's switch of labels was more than mere dissatisfaction on his part; Warners were annoyed at having lost James Taylor to CBS and saw their acquisition of Paul Simon as a considerable feather in their cap. Apparently Simon still owed CBS one album, and was keen to record an album of other people's material to appease his old label.

Sadly, the project, which Simon envisaged as an album's worth of duets – Bruce Springsteen, James Taylor and Billy Joel were among artists approached – never materialised, and the CBS obligation was met with the release of a *Greatest Hits* package in 1977.

Paul Simon had an unequalled reputation in the world of popular music, even Simon and Garfunkel's harshest critics would admit his craftsmanlike approach to songwriting. But the **One Trick Pony** project was a whole new ball game. Simon had written little prose since his college days, and the problems of mounting a film by someone with no cinematic track record were manifold. To gain some experience before the cameras, Simon undertook a cameo role in Woody Allen's **Annie Hall** in 1977. Simon's role went largely unnoticed, although his billing was sizable. His portrayal of a smug, superficial LA personality was harshly accurate. Simon also appeared again on **Saturday Night Live** with his friend, actor Elliot Gould, dressed in a turkey suit! He also indulged in another piece of self-deprecation when he appeared in Eric Idle's Beatles spoof, **The Rutles**. Simon was interviewed, along with Mick Jagger, talking earnestly about the "Pre-Fab Four". Simon remembered straight-faced, attending a Rabbi Shankar gig with Stig O'Hara, and denied that the Rutles had influenced his work in any way whatsoever!

While Simon studied song composition, and laboured over the script for **One Trick Pony**, the only two new songs to appear during his five year absence were included on a *Greatest Hits Etc.* package.

Slip Slidin' Away was a captivating song, which featured the gospel quartet, the Oak Ridge Boys. The song's beguiling melody belied the bitterness of the lyrics, the illusion that "we're gliding down the highway/When, in fact, we're slip slidin' away." The idea that one draws nearer one's dreams as we get older is denied by Simon. "A bad day's when I lie in bed/And think of things that might have been" is a rueful acceptance by someone who is denied the safety of illusion.

The third verse sounds definitely autobiographical, the father kissing his sleeping son, before returning to his own home. Simon's ex-wife Peggy had custody of their only child, and although Simon saw him as often as possible, he obviously missed not having him with him all the time.

Stranded In A Limousine is a faster, funkier number. A jazzy detour into New York's mean streets, about a mobster, who'd left his neighbourhood, "like a rattlesnake sheds its skin", and who avoids any unwanted police attention. It's a punchy song, with a crisp horn arrangement by Simon, a minor addition to his canon, but welcome nonetheless. The live version of *American Tune* on the album was previously unavailable, featuring Simon with a string quartet. It was a tastefully compiled album, and one which showed just how much Simon's music had broadened from his S&G days. Simon admitted he felt he had "proved" himself when *Still Crazy* picked up a Grammy Award in 1975, proving finally that he could stand in his own right away from the shadow of Simon and Garfunkel.

Simon explained his reasons for undertaking **One Trick Pony** to Dave Marsh, in a Rolling Stone interview of October 1980: "I wanted to do something other than just record an album. I felt my choices were either to write a Broadway show or a movie. I chose the movie because I thought it would be closer to the process of recording. You get a take, and that's your take. I don't have to go in every night to see whether the cast is performing. Also, I could still record and use the movie as a score. But if I'd written a show, I couldn't have recorded my own stuff – other people would have had to sing it."

Simon felt he needed the sort of challenge a film posed. After years of success in his chosen field (he had accrued 12 Grammy awards and royalties from *Bridge* alone assured that he was a very rich man). He was also aware of the limitations imposed by the pop song. Much as he tried to change his approach to writing, whether with unorthodox song structures, in composition or arrangement, Paul Simon felt up to undertaking the rigours imposed by a film. With his novel postponed indefinitely, **One Trick Pony** became a sort of personal Everest for him. Simon told David Robson of the Sunday Times: "I felt nervous about it, but I wanted to feel nervous . . . that's what I call 'the good scared', where you bite off more than you can chew, and learn to chew bigger!"

There were, of course, problems. Simon couldn't convince himself that he would be good enough to play Jonah Levin, the film's central character, yet he was reluctant to entrust the role to a non-singing actor. Simon toyed with the idea of using Gary Busey, who had been so convincing in **The Buddy Holly Story**, and at one time broached the idea with Academy Award winner Richard Dreyfuss, but "it couldn't be done . . . There was no way that Dreyfuss could be in the movie and open his mouth and have *my* voice come out." Feeling that scoring, writing and starring in the film would stretch him sufficiently,

Simon engaged a young director Robert M. Young. The film's budget of around six million dollars was supplied by Warners, with the understanding that this hinged on Simon's commitment to the project.

Consequentially, the finished film was unfairly handled by Warner Bros. It only received limited distribution in the States, and Holland was the only country to officially see it in Europe. **One Trick Pony** has surfaced on cable television in America and Simon has even talked of buying it back from Warners, but it remains largely unseen.

Maybe Warners were expecting a 'sex and drugs and rock and roll and scandal' type of film, which was far from Simon's original intention. Maybe they weren't happy with the fact that the Jonah Levin character was such a loser. Whatever their reasons, it is a shame the film didn't receive wider distribution.

One Trick Pony is flawed but it is one of the few films from a major studio to treat the rock lifestyle seriously, particularly coming from someone like Paul Simon who intuitively understood the business. Simon was understandably miffed at Warners attitude: "People ask you 'isn't it about time to stop playing rock 'n' roll?' Yet nobody ever tells Stanley Kubrick 'You're 51, now isn't it time to stop?' . . . I wanted to make a statement about the record industry which didn't fit into a three minute pop song. The industry has been taken over by accountants and lawyers, which is a shame. You need people in it who like music."

That is the message at the heart of **One Trick Pony**. It's a wry, compassionate film about an ageing rock star, Jonah Levin, who still wants to rock 'n' roll, but is made only too aware that he's pushing forty. It's a paean to those with the rock 'n' roll in their blood, who can't shake the habit, who can never hang up their rock 'n' roll shoes. It's almost an epitaph for a generation, for those who never made it. On one of the songs on the soundtrack, Jonah sings: "Here's to all the boys who came along/Carrying soft guitars in cardboard cases . . . Do you wonder where those boys have gone?" They've gone on to become like Jonah Levin, who can't rid himself of the rock 'n' roll bug, but knows that his historical hour has long since past.

As someone whose career has been blessed with the Midas touch, the character Simon plays in the film could well be the other side of the coin. Jonah Levin could well be Paul Simon, if *The Sounds Of Silence* had simply been a one-off hit, and Simon found himself on those sad tour packages, where Sixties stars play their one hit and just jog a few memories before moving on to the next town. Indeed, in the film, Simon allows himself that luxury of speculation. As Jonah, he takes part in a *Salute To The Sixties* night, along with Tiny Tim and the Lovin' Spoonful, and Jonah sings a one-dimensional, anti-war protest song called *Soft Parachutes*. As if saying there but for the grace of Tiny Tim goes Paul Simon! In a sense, it's also a valediction to the Sixties, to an era of a special kind of innocence.

The film is rich in dry, laconic East Coast humour, as in the scene where Jonah confronts an unsympathetic programmer, the man with "Twenty years of AM Ears", who figures that only the Stones and Springsteen "successfully combine music and spectacle." "How about Albert Schweitzer?" queries Jonah. "You know, Africa, the organ, disease. Albert Schweitzer, the king of music and spectacle!" "What label's he on?"

Paul Simon attends "Lunch Hour" première on Broadway. December 1980

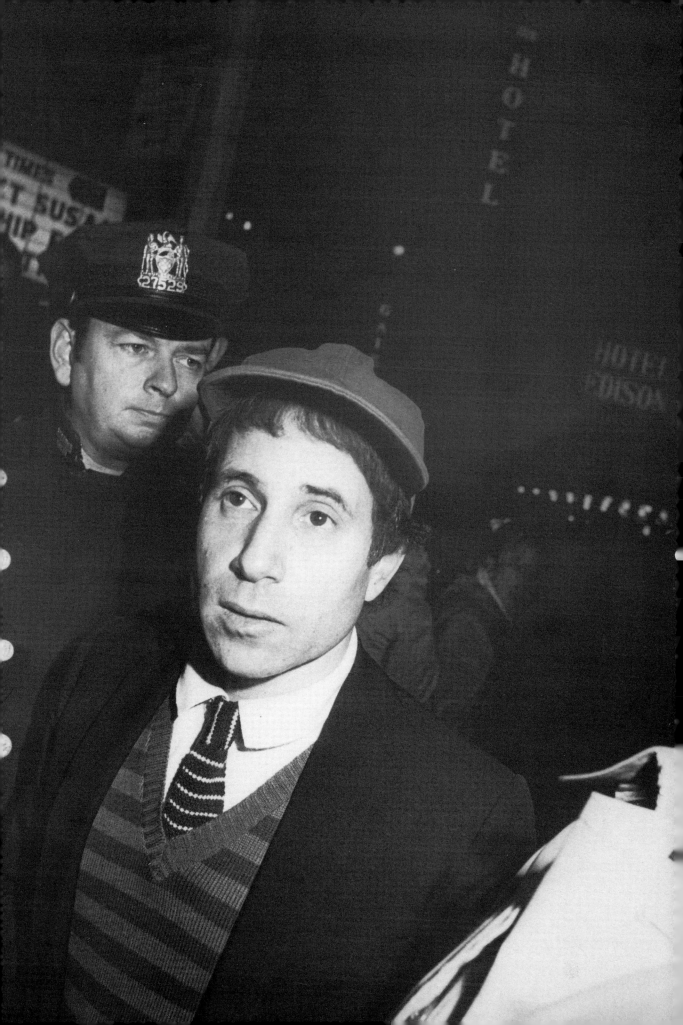

Simon's knowledge of – and belief in – rock 'n' roll runs through the film. From the evocative opening montage that accompanies *Late In The Evening*, to the casting of Lou Reed as Jonah's unscrupulous record producer. The changing musical climate is tellingly indicated early on, as Jonah's band punch out a blistering set at the Agora Ballroom, Ohio, only to be upstaged by the obviously younger, new wave B52s. Simon's envious, uncomprehending glance as they perform says so much about that generation gap.

The spirit of Elvis Presley hovers over the film. Early on, Jonah's wife tells him: "You have wanted to be Elvis Presley since you were thirteen years old. Well it's not a goal that you're likely to achieve. He didn't do too well with it himself." Later on, Jonah and his band are on the road, and in the tour bus they're betting on how many dead rock stars they can name. Hendrix, Joplin, Cochran are reeled off, and Elvis's name invariably crops up. "Yeah", remarks Jonah wistfully, "he's dead." Simon told Melody Maker's Ray Coleman: "The rock 'n' roll solo performer was defined by Elvis Presley, the quintessential rock 'n' roll star. I am eight or nine inches too short to try that whole thing." And to Dave Marsh: "I *loved* Elvis Presley. And I said to myself 'I can never, *never* be Elvis Presley . . .!'"

Jonah Levin eventually reconciles himself with his estranged wife by quoting her the Presley monlogue from *Are You Lonesome Tonight?* It's a scene that reminded me of Woody Allen's character at the end of **Play It Again, Sam** sincerely imploring Diane Keaton to get on the plane and rejoin her husband. "That's beautiful" murmurs Keaton. "They're the closing lines from **Casablanca** says Woody, "I've waited my whole life to say them!" Tiny Jewish Paul Simon realised early on he could never *be* Elvis Presley, **One Trick Pony** is his monument to prove that he *tried* though.

Autobiographical elements pepper the film but, as with his songs, they are only a part of Paul Simon. Simon was keen to stress that the film was a work of fiction, which, of course, didn't stop people interpreting it as autobiographical. But then that's what happens when an established rock star makes a film about another rock star. **One Trick Pony** is a compassionate film about rock 'n' roll, and as such was considerably more successful than other films of the genre, like Willie Nelson's cliché-ridden **Honeysuckle Rose** or Dylan's rambling **Renaldo And Clara**.

The Los Angeles Times called it: "An exceptionally handsome movie . . . an intimate film of much wit, style and impact. It ranks as one of the year's best." Which must have encouraged Simon, although he was obviously unhappy with Warners handling of the film once it was completed: "My feeling at the time was, well, I've made a failure. I hadn't had a big history of failure; I'd had a pretty good history of success. And here was this project that I'd put more effort into than any other project I'd ever done. I had a lot of years tied up in it, and it came and went just like that."

The subsequent soundtrack album was released with a suitable barrage of publicity, drawing attention to the fact that it was Simon's first album of original material in five years. Critical and public reaction was reserved, despite the fact that it *was* a new Paul Simon album and the soundtrack from a film few people had seen, or were likely to see. Consequentially, few of the songs stood up out of context although Simon told many journalists that it was the one album of his with which he was most satisfied. But a lot had happened in the intervening five years, music had changed, and there was little indication on the **One Trick Pony** album that Simon was aware of those changes.

The single, *Late In The Evening* was a rousing taster, and managed to scrape into the charts. It apparently started out as a studio jam, with Simon and his band playing around with Presley's version of Junior Parker's *Mystery Train*, and it grew from there. The song is propelled along by Steve Gadd's thunderous drumming, and features some typically idiosyncratic Simon rhymes. I love the second verse, which vividly portrays the young Simon "with his troops" out on the street: "And I heard the sound of acapella groups/Singing late in the evening/And all the girls out on the stoops." When performed live, the song grows stronger and stronger, and was one of the highlights of the Central Park reunion.

That's Why God Made The Movies plays over scenes with Jonah Levin and his son, and the final verse refers to François Truffaut's **L'Enfant Sauvage** film, about a young boy allegedly brought up by wolves in eighteenth century France. *One Trick Pony* is a live song, with a typically acute Paul Simon line in "It's the principal source of his revenue". The album's best ballad is the beautiful *How The Heart Approaches What It Yearns*, with its enticing, atmospheric opening lines: "In the blue light of the Belvedere Motel/Wondering, as the television burns/How the heart approaches what it yearns." It's a song Simon himself was particularly proud of, commenting on the unorthodox time signature "I don't expect other people to notice it. But at least *I* know it."

The remainder of the songs fit perfectly into the film, but are less successful when isolated on the album. **One Trick Pony** at least proved Paul Simon hadn't been idle during his five year absence from the public eye but people just expected more than this patchy album.

Simon agreed to tour to promote the album and to generate interest in the film. He also made himself widely available for interviews, mainly to promote the film, but invariably found himself drawn back to his former glories, and the chances of a reconciliation with Garfunkel. The most embarrassing encounter came on the BBC's **Old Grey Whistle Test**, with Ann Nightingale doggedly insisting that it must be very difficult for Simon to write songs since he split from Garfunkel! "We never wrote any songs together. I wrote all the songs. Not wanting to sound immodest, but Art only *sang* them with me." But Ms Nightingale wouldn't let go, and wondered just how many people actually *knew* this. "I guess everyone except you" responded Simon.

I saw Simon towards the end of that European tour, at the Hammersmith Odeon. It had been five years since I'd last seen him at the London Palladium, and my musical tastes had changed considerably during those years. I remember that it was more out of a sense of duty that I went along, never expecting that the old magic would sparkle again. I came away with my faith restored in Paul Simon and his music. Whilst there was none of the immediacy of rock 'n' roll, Simon stood head and shoulders above many of the rock writers that had sprung up in his wake. Apparently, Simon had had his band in the theatre soundchecking since 10 am, and it was worth the effort, every instrument, every voice was perfectly balanced, enhancing the songs, and setting a standard few other performers could attain.

Simon drew on his familiar songs, but also intergrated the strongest of his new songs into his set. It was a superb evening, in the company of a master musician, an evening of finely-crafted music from a writer who will transcend fluctuating fashion. In these days, Simon may appear closer to the cocktail elegance of Noel Coward than the street polemics of Joe Strummer, but it is our good luck that Simon chose rock as his medium.

Unfortunately, I wasn't at the last night of the European tour at Hammersmith, when Simon voiced his thanks to the audience, and said he only wished there was some way he could repay them. "Buy us a drink then" some wag shouted from the balcony, and to everyone's surprise, he did. Paul Simon stood the Hammersmith Odeon a round, which didn't leave him much change from £1,000!

Talking to Melody Maker's Ray Coleman, Simon revealed that he had moved further away from direct political comment in his songs. He said he was not inspired to write a song about the newly-elected Ronald Reagan, as he had been to write *American Tune* about Richard Nixon. It was an unsettling comment from a writer who had so capably reflected the American liberal attitude in his work, particularly in the light of Reagan's avowed hawkishness, and America's growing involvement in El Salvador. As a writer, though, Simon has proved his ability at distancing himself from a topic before writing about it. His work is obviously affected by his personal emotions and he is a prolific reader. Events or personalities may not suggest themselves immediately for a song, but are instead stockpiled in Simon's mental filing system for future reference. Simon also went to some length in demystifying the image which had surrounded him for years: "Several myths surround me, and one is that I'm a recluse, never leave my home in New York, write miserable songs and don't smile! I'm not sad at all, although everyone is depressed at some time in their life. I go out and meet people, and smile."

Although Simon's tour marked a triumphant return, the album and film of **One Trick Pony** were nowhere near as successful as they might have been. With Garfunkel's career(s) in neutral, Simon had begun seeing his former partner again on a fairly regular basis. Gradually, after eleven years of bad feeling, lack of communication and musical separation plus the prompting of mutual friends, Simon and Garfunkel drifted back together again.

Chapter Nine

Whatever the personal reasons for getting back together again (on what seems like a relatively permanent basis), Simon and Garfunkel were aided by the unlikely combination of the Rolling Stones and a sportswear firm. Many of the Sixties stalwarts had fallen by the wayside. Dylan's triumphant return in 1978 had been marred by the poor music which accompanied his later Christian 'rebirth'. The Beatles, even before John Lennon's tragic murder, were never likely to perform together again. American rock 'n' roll, while roaring ahead with Springsteen at its helm, was still trailing the dead weight of anonymous bands like Journey, Foreigner and Styx. It took the Stones to remind people of the pulling power of a guaranteed rock legend. Their 1981 American tour was the most successful in rock history (one day's tee shirt sales in San Francisco alone netted over a million dollars!) The fact which surprised many people was that the majority of people who actually went to see the Stones were kids who weren't even born when they were first around. They were out to see a rock 'n' roll legend, perhaps for the last time.

While Simon and Garfunkel's fans had kept pace with their respective solo careers, they still craved the magical combination of Simon *and* Garfunkel. That partnership proved irresistible, and provided the mass appeal. Nostalgia was proving all the more marketable as the world lurched hesitantly into a new decade. With the Beatles little more than a potent memory, Dylan a Christian recluse and the Stones proving there was a growing market available, the timing couldn't have been better for a Simon and Garfunkel reunion.

Paul Simon has always been vehemently partisan about his home city of New York, and willingly agreed to play a solo concert in Central Park in the autumn of 1981, when approached by Warren Hirsh of Fiorucci Sportswear, who had previously promoted similar shows in the park by James Taylor and Elton John. Simon was keen on the idea, and approached Garfunkel to come and join him onstage for the second half of the show. But as Garfunkel recalled the situation to Rolling Stone in 1981: "Some friends of ours said why not a full Simon and Garfunkel concert? That would give the crowd the biggest kick. It also didn't seem right to either of us that Paul should be the opening act for Simon and Garfunkel." The inevitability of the situation was apparent, and the duo began sounding each other out at rehearsal and in conversation. The announcement of a full time reunion may have seemed too much like an admission of failure. "It got easy again", said Simon, "Artie and I had some heart-to-heart

EBET ROBERTS

The Reunion Concert in
Central Park, September
1981

Amid rumours of a reunion
for an album, S&G make a
rare appearance together at
NY's Underground disco

Overleaf: Art & Paul attend
a party at the Savoy to
celebrate the reunion
concert – Paul with
girlfriend Carrie Fisher and
Artie with Penny Marshall
(of *Lavern & Shirley*)

DAVID McGOUGH/DMI

talks, which, amazingly, we had never had, and we just settled some
things . . . We found ourselves talking about what would work,
instead of what the other person did that was wrong."

Both men had just turned forty, were upset by the response to their
recent solo projects, realised the possibilities, both creative and
financial, that a reunion could bring and started thinking seriously
about the idea. Hanging out together, all the old antagonisms were
soon forgotten. The realisation that they had as much in common as
had kept them previously apart was soon realised. "We reminded
ourselves of the humour we shared, the jokes, the similar concerns –
the similarity of our lives" Garfunkel recalled.

It may have made perfect sense for the two of them. The rest of the
world was slightly more cynical about Simon and Garfunkel's

WALTER McBRIDE/RETNA LTD

Art leaving the Broadway
play **Amadeus** – August 1981

motives for reforming. The relative failure of their recent solo efforts, the enormous financial possibilities a reunion would bring to them both, the security of Simon *and* Garfunkel, a chance to test the reaction in their home town. These were some of the reactions news of their reunion brought, which Simon was swift to dismiss: "The truth is, neither Artie nor I feel our lives rise and fall on hit albums or flop albums . . . I don't think we'd get together if the potential for a joyous reunion weren't there. We'd never decide to grit our teeth just

Concert at Wembley,
London in June 1982

to make a couple of million dollars." Maybe not, and how comforting to be in a position to be able to say that.

September 19, 1981 was the date set for the reunion. The stage was built resembling the New York skyline, and the event cost around 750,000 dollars to stage, with Simon putting up the bulk of the money. Large crowds were expected, but the size of the half million crowd surprised everyone. The days of the big festival, with a crowd of that size gathering to see one act, had long since past. They came in their

117

At a press conference in
London – Spring 1982

ANDRE CSILLAG

Warner Bros. Records
promo. pic.

WARNER BROS. RECORDS

hundreds of thousands not simply to a concert, but to celebrate the passing of time, and see if some of it could be snatched back.

It was a chill, autumn evening when Mayor Ed Koch came onstage around dusk and announced simply: "Ladies and gentlemen, Simon and Garfunkel." The roars which greeted the two tiny figures were deafening, the city of New York paying tribute to two of its celebrated sons.

"It's great to do a neighbourhood concert" cracked Simon early on and the crowd roared their enthusiasm, paying tribute to the duo they wished had never gone away. It was an emotional occasion, a celebration of lost innocence. Simon and Garfunkel's rapturous reception was a testimony that, "after changes upon changes/we are more or less the same." That the turmoil of the intervening years was a bad dream, like Cambodia and Watergate had never happened. After eleven years, Simon and Garfunkel's Central Park concert was like the return of 'Joltin' Joe' DiMaggio.

The success of the Central Park show generated an enormous amount of interest in Simon and Garfunkel. CBS quickly compiled *The Simon And Garfunkel Collection*. "Seventeen of their all time greatest recordings which no-one's record collection will be complete without" boasted their old company. (Indeed, so swiftly was the the album put together in Britain, there were strong rumours that the hazy couple on the cover were not Simon and Garfunkel, simply a couple of lookalikes photographed somewhere on the Welsh Coast! It was a rumour CBS swiftly denied.) Nonetheless, the album arrived just in time for Christmas, and sold close on two million copies in Europe. There were no new songs, nor indeed any live versions of old songs on the album, so the sales indicated that, like the Stones, Simon and Garfunkel had reached a whole new generation of fans.

Simon attained an intellectual accolade in 1980, when the revised Penguin Dictionary Of Modern Quotations included four of his lyrics. Simon was sandwiched between surrealist playwright N.F. Simpson and Frank Silver, author of *Yes, We Have No Bananas*, an irony I am sure he would appreciate.

The subsequent, obligatory live double album of the Central Park show offered a hint of the event. Yet few of the familiar S&G songs are enhanced by the record, *Kodachrome* loses its dramatic drive, *America, Homeward Bound* and *The Boxer* are perfunctorily performed, and Garfunkel even manages to fluff the second verse of *Bridge Over Troubled Water*. The songs which worked best were those which had previously been solo Simon efforts, a funkier *Slip Slidin' Away*, a thunderous *Late In The Evening* and a haunting *American Tune* all benefitted from Garfunkel's harmonising. His solo renderings of *April Come She Will* and *Scarborough Fair* are spellbinding.

The only 'new' songs are another excursion into the Everly Brothers back catalogue, and personally I find S&G's version of *Wake Up Little Susie* plain embarrassing, two 40 year old men wondering how their parents are going to react when they're late home from a date! Chuck Berry's automotive tribute, *Maybelline*, fares better, but adds little of real quality to the Simon and Garfunkel repertoire. A major disappointment is that room wasn't found on the album for Simon's only new song, *The Late, Great Johnny Ace*, a potted history of rock 'n' roll, and one of Simon's most touching,

Overleaf: Playing alone on giant encyclopaedia page

Art in '81

Paul Simon with his wife, Peggy not long before the birth of their son, Harper

obviously autobiographical songs.

Johnny Ace was a young R&B singer, who had a posthumous Top 20 hit in 1955 with *Pledging My Love*. Ace died backstage on Christmas Eve 1954, after losing at Russian roulette. Simon's poignant tribute recalls Ace and conjures up the Beatles, Stones and John Lennon by name. The most chilling moment of the show came during Simon's performance, when, at the exact moment he invoked Lennon's name, a fan leapt onstage and rushed towards him. The look on Simon's face was of anguish, and terror, like thinking maybe *he* is the next to go, in front of half a million fans within a gunshot of the Dakota Building.

Simon was haunted for days afterwards, with the kid's words ringing in his ears: "Paul, I need to talk to you." That was how much Simon and Garfunkel meant to their millions of fans. It was a thin line between Mark Chapman and John Lennon, and between Paul Simon, and that unknown young man who *had* to speak to the man

whose songs had reflected his life. The fact that it happened during Simon's tribute to another rock legend was eerie, the grey area between reality and illusion. An area that Paul Simon had so suitably evoked in his songs. Those songs which will ring down the years, suitable to the mood the listener wants, the mood Paul Simon helps create, because *he* understands.

So, 1982 brings Simon and Garfunkel together again, with talk of a new studio album, their first since *Bridge Over Troubled Water*. Their appearances this summer will mean millions of people will have the opportunity to relive a little bit of their past. Those haunting voices will harmonise again on Simon's marvellous songs, and the thousands gathered before their idols will scream for a song about the inability to communicate. And once again, Simon and Garfunkel will sing *The Sounds Of Silence*. And everyone will remember where they were when they first heard that song, and how their lives, and our lives, have changed since. And we will be comfortable in that shared memory. That is perhaps the real tribute to Simon and Garfunkel.

Discography

Albums

Simon and Garfunkel
Wednesday Morning 3AM (CBS 63370, 1964. UK, 1968)
Sounds Of Silence (CBS 62690, 1966)
Parsley, Sage, Rosemary And Thyme (CBS 62860, 1966)
The Graduate (CBS 70042, 1968)
Bookends (CBS 63101, 1968)
Bridge Over Troubled Water (CBS 63699, 1970)
Simon And Garfunkel's Greatest Hits (CBS 69003, 1972)
The Simon And Garfunkel Collection (CBS 10029, 1981)
The Concert In Central Park (Geffen 96008, 1982)

Paul Simon
The Paul Simon Songbook (CBS 62579, 1965)
Paul Simon (CBS 69007, 1972)
There Goes Rhymin' Simon (CBS 69035, 1973)
Live Rhymin' (CBS 69059, 1974)
Still Crazy After All These Years (CBS 86001, 1975)
Greatest Hits, Etc. (CBS 10007, 1977)
One Trick Pony (Warner Bros. K56846, 1980)

Art Garfunkel
Angel Clare (CBS 69021, 1973)
Breakaway (CBS 86002, 1975)
Watermark (CBS 86054, 1978)
Fate For Breakfast (CBS 86082, 1979)
Scissors Cut (CBS 85259, 1981)

Singles

Simon and Garfunkel
The Sound Of Silence 1965
Homeward Bound 1966 (reissued 1976)
I Am A Rock 1966
The Dangling Conversation 1966
A Hazy Shade Of Winter 1966
At The Zoo 1967
Fakin' It 1967

Scarborough Fair 1968
Mrs Robinson 1968 (reissued 1982 on Geffen)
The Boxer 1969
Bridge Over Troubled Water 1970 (reissued 1978)
Cecilia 1970
Keep The Customer Satisfied 1970
America 1972
My Little Town 1975 (all on CBS)
Wake Up Little Susie 1982 (Geffen)

Paul Simon
He Was My Brother 1964 (Oriole, as Jerry Landis)
I Am A Rock 1965
Mother And Child Reunion 1972
Me And Julio Down By The Schoolyard 1972
Take Me To The Mardi Gras 1973
Loves Me Like A Rock 1973
American Tune 1974
Sound Of Silence 1974
Something So Right 1974
Gone At Last 1975
50 Ways To Leave Your Lover 1976
Still Crazy After All These Years 1976
Stranded In A Limousine 1978 (all on CBS)
Late In the Evening 1980 (Warner Bros)
One Trick Pony 1980
Oh Marion 1981 (Warner Bros)

Art Garfunkel
All I Know 1973
I Shall Sing 1974
Second Avenue 1974
I Only Have Eyes For You 1975
Breakaway 1976
I Believe When I Fall In Love 1976
We Are Going 1976
Crying In My Sleep 1977
(What A) Wonderful World 1978
Marionette 1978
Bright Eyes 1979
Since I Don't Have You 1979
Heart In New York 1981
Scissors Cut 1981